PALMERSTON

1784
–1865

British History in Perspective
General Editor: Jeremy Black

Eugenio Biagini *Gladstone*
D. G. Boyce *The Irish Question and British Politics, 1868–1996* (2nd edn)
Keith M. Brown *Kingdom or Province? Scotland and the Regal Union, 1603–1715*
A. D. Carr *Medieval Wales*
Eveline Cruickshanks *The Glorious Revolution*
Anne Curry *The Hundred Years War*
Susan Doran *England and Europe in the Sixteenth Century*
Seán Duffy *Ireland in the Middle Ages*
David Gladstone *The Twentieth-Century Welfare State*
Brian Golding *Conquest and Colonisation: the Normans in Britain, 1066–1100*
Sean Greenwood *Britain and the Cold War, 1945–1991*
David Harkness *Ireland in the Twentieth Century: Divided Island*
Ann Hughes *The Causes of the English Civil War* (2nd edn)
Ronald Hutton *The British Republic, 1649–1660* (2nd edn)
T. A. Jenkins *Disraeli and Victorian Conservatism*
T. A. Jenkins *Sir Robert Peel*
H. S. Jones *Victorian Political Thought*
Christine Kinealy *The Great Irish Famine*
D. E. Kennedy *The English Revolution, 1642–1649*
John F. McCaffrey *Scotland in the Nineteenth Century*
A. P. Martinich *Thomas Hobbes*
W. M. Ormrod *Political Life in Medieval England, 1300–1450*
Richie Ovendale *Anglo-American Relations in the Twentieth Century*
Ian Packer *Lloyd George*
Keith Perry *British Politics and the American Revolution*
Murray G. H. Pittock *Jacobitism*
A. J. Pollard *The Wars of the Roses*
David Powell *British Politics and the Labour Question, 1868–1990*
Richard Rex *Henry VIII and the English Reformation*
G. R. Searle *The Liberal Party: Triumph and Disintegration, 1886–1929* (2nd edn)
John Stuart Shaw *The Political History of Eighteenth-Century Scotland*
W. M. Spellman *John Locke*
William Stafford *John Stuart Mill*
Bruce Webster *Medieval Scotland*
Ann Williams *Kingship and Government in Pre-Conquest England*
Ian S. Wood *Churchill*
John W. Young *Britain and European Unity, 1945–1999* (2nd edn)
Paul R. Ziegler *Palmerston*

Please note that a sister series, *Social History in Perspective*, is now available, covering key topics in social and cultural history.

British History in Perspective
Series Standing Order
ISBN 0–333–71356–7 hardcover
ISBN 0–333–69331–0 paperback

You can receive future titles in this series as they are published by placing a standing order. Please contact your bookseller or, in case of difficulty, write to the address below with your name and address, the title of the series and the ISBN quoted above.
Customer Services Department, Macmillan Distribution Ltd
Houndmills, Basingstoke, Hampshire RG21 6XS, England

wcastle City Library

one 0191 277 4100

ormation@newcastle.gov.uk

rrowing

er   Mr James Wankowicz

en Fees   GBP 0.00

	Due Date
Baldwin	05/08/10
Disraeli	05/08/10
Palmerston	05/08/10
David & Winston : ho\	05/08/10
Petain	05/08/10

08.07.2010 12:24:05

ank you for using the new City Library

PALMERSTON

PAUL R. ZIEGLER

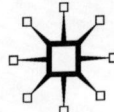

© Paul R. Ziegler 2003

All rights reserved. No reproduction, copy or transmission of this publication may be made without written permission.

No paragraph of this publication may be reproduced, copied or transmitted save with written permission or in accordance with the provisions of the Copyright, Designs and Patents Act 1988, or under the terms of any licence permitting limited copying issued by the Copyright Licensing Agency, 90 Tottenham Court Road, London W1T 4LP.

Any person who does any unauthorized act in relation to this publication may be liable to criminal prosecution and civil claims for damages.

The authors has asserted his right to be identified as the author of this work in accordance with the Copyright, Designs and Patents Act 1988.

First published 2003 by
PALGRAVE MACMILLAN
Houndmills, Basingstoke, Hampshire RG21 6XS and
175 Fifth Avenue, New York, N.Y. 10010
Companies and representatives throughout the world

PALGRAVE MACMILLAN is the new global academic imprint of the Palgrave Macmillan division of St. Martin's Press, LLC and of Palgrave Macmillan Ltd. Macmillan® is a registered trademark in the United States, United Kingdom and other countries. Palgrave is a registered trademark in the European Union and other countries.

ISBN 0–333–67625–4 hardback
ISBN 0–333–67626–2 paperback

This book is printed on paper suitable for recycling and made from fully managed and sustained forest sources.

A catalogue record for this book is available from the British Library.

Library of Congress Cataloging-in-Publication Data
Ziegler, Paul R.
  Palmerston / Paul R. Ziegler.
    p. cm.—(British history in perspective)
  Includes bibliographical references and index.
  ISBN 0–333–67625–4—ISBN 0–333–67626–2 (pbk.)
  1. Palmerston, Henry John Temple, Viscount, 1784–1865.
  2. Great Britain—Politics and government—1837–1901.
  3. Prime ministers—Great Britain—Biography. I. Title.
  II. British history in perspective (Palgrave Macmillan (Firm))

DA536.P2 Z54 2002
941.081′092—dc21
[B]   2002072339

10 9 8 7 6 5 4 3 2 1
12 11 10 09 08 07 06 05 04 03

Printed in China

For Chris and Mayumi

Contents

Acknowledgements viii

Introduction 1

1 The Making of a Canningite 7

2 Interests but no Entanglements 29

3 The Revolutionary Challenge 55

4 Politics without Party 78

5 The Last Years 105

Conclusion 129

Notes 135
Bibliography 147
Index 151

ACKNOWLEDGEMENTS

Historical enquiry is by its very nature a collaborative enterprise, so great is the debt owed to the contributions of others. Since good scholarship tends to beget good scholarship, I must acknowledge all those whose trenchant studies have illuminated Palmerston's life. I am especially indebted to those trustees, archivists and librarians who have provided me with access to the vast holdings in Palmerston materials. I must thank, in particular, the Trustees of the Broadlands Archive Trust for permission to use the Palmerston Papers at the University of Southampton Library. I am especially indebted to the archivists at Southampton, Christopher Woolgar, Karen Robson and their staff, for the uncommon courtesy and assistance afforded me while using the Palmerston Papers. In addition, my thanks goes to all owners and custodians of other manuscript sources listed in the bibliography, especially those at the National Register of Archives, the Department of Manuscripts in the British Library, and other institutions. The Public Record Office papers are crown copyright.

On a more personal note, I am deeply in debt to Jeremy Black for his helpful suggestions, wise counsel and support for this project. In addition, it would be remiss of me not to thank Assumption College for its financial assistance and sabbatical leaves, without which this enterprise would not have flourished. Special recognition must also be given to my colleagues, Provost Mary Lou Anderson, Dean Mary Kielbasa, Professor Kenneth Moynihan, Suzanne Lewandowski and Carol Maksian, whose readiness to assist me was unfailingly generous. Finally, I owe a special debt to my son, Professor Christopher Ziegler, whose critical reading of this text has been perceptive, sharp and enormously constructive.

Assumption College   PAUL R. ZIEGLER

INTRODUCTION

Implicit in *The Times*' comment that the death of Lord Palmerston in 1865 was the end of an era, was the recognition that he placed his stamp upon nineteenth-century Britain. This judgement seems at odds with the fact that Henry John Temple, Third Viscount Palmerston, was a genuine product of the eighteenth century, marked in almost every way by his aristocratic lineage. Born to privilege, he was an absentee Irish landlord as well as an owner of major landholdings in Britain. He thoroughly enjoyed the leisurely life of turf, travel and gala balls that accompanied his rank. But this same rank set him apart from the lower orders whose power would be released by the twin forces of the Industrial and French Revolutions. His aristocratic connections gave him entry to a seat in the House of Commons in 1806 as well as a sinecure position in the Admiralty.

On the face of it, Palmerston appeared to be an anachronism in the century that followed. He never denied his Tory roots and he seemed uncertain of himself in responding to the rising tide of liberalism and nationalism as the nineteenth century opened clamorously. Was it simply a matter of luck, physical endurance and persistence that explains his powerful presence in the nineteenth century? To suggest that Palmerston was merely marking time would be to ignore his more than 50 years of public service, which included two terms as Prime Minister (1855–8, 1859–65), sixteen years as Foreign Secretary, and three years in the Home Office.

Despite his eighteenth-century roots, the historical Palmerston is remembered as the very personification of nineteenth-century England. His brimming self-confidence in Britain's greatness and his unhesitating willingness to advertise his nation's virtues to the rest of the world and to identify himself with the British people made him their natural spokesman. Indeed, most historians would agree that the nineteenth century would be incomprehensible without reference to this man of seeming contradictions. This short biography will re-assess Palmerston's defining impact on his age in an effort to reconcile these contradictions and determine whether the paradoxes within him mirrored the complex incongruities of the age.

Several currents ran through Palmerston's public life which illuminate our understanding of the man and his policies. Given his aristocratic upbringing, he was apt to defend order and suspect change. Still, although often uncommitted to wholesale reform, there were signs that he evolved as a pragmatic politician open to change. As a follower of the liberal Tory George Canning, he had a mixed record of suppressing riotous outbursts while seeking to defuse revolution with reform measures. After the Peterloo riots of 1819, he favoured the repressive Six Acts and did not hesitate to arm his servants against rioters. In these years of popular unrest over the state of the economy and the call for parliamentary reform and retrenchment, Palmerston became the target of Radical attacks for being associated with the Liverpool government. However, as events moved apace in the 1820s and divisions grew between Canningites and High Tories in the Liverpool ministry, Palmerston began to show his reformist colours. For example, although not for the immediate abolition of slavery in the colonies, he favoured its gradual elimination. As the issue of Catholic Emancipation was advanced in the late 1820s he became its champion. Finally, his position on parliamentary reform had extended beyond a piecemeal approach of granting representation to large cities to his support for the Whigs' 1832 measures. This signalled his alliance with the Whigs and his effective conversion from Canningite to Whig.

The emergence of Palmerston as a liberal thereafter follows an uneven path. In 1832, he admitted that his support for the Whigs' Reform Bill was unenthusiastic. Like Macaulay, he believed that abuses had to be reformed to allay the dangers of revolution. Only as long as rank, property rights and order were maintained, could reform be risked. Given this tepid approach to reform while still supporting despotic rules in this early stage of his career, Palmerston not surprisingly remained a constant target of radical attacks. If one sees, as some historians do, that Palmerston acted as a brake upon the movement of political and social progress, then one might conclude that true reform would be impossible until after his death in 1865. Similarly, it could be said that he demagogically exploited class differences to safeguard his own aristocratic preserve. A more benign observation would be that Palmerston was essentially a pragmatic politician who fixed problems according to his ability to solve them. In short, while never a liberal in theory, he was one in practice.

To test this characterization of him as a practical liberal requires a review of his record during the reform era. An examination of the 1830s and 1840s, during which time he drifted over to the Whig side, shows that he was an ardent foe of the slave trade, espoused the New Poor Law, and favoured legislation that alleviated the miserable conditions affecting the working classes. At the same time, he earnestly favoured the suppression of public disorder and he became a steadfast critic of radicals such as Cobden and Bright. Yet years later the truest test of his liberal credentials came when reformers of different stripes looked to him as their leader in the formation of the modern Liberal Party.

If Palmertston is accused of dragging his feet in advancing domestic reforms, his reputation preceded him for his relentless advocacy of constitutional liberalism abroad. As the man who helped shape British diplomacy from 1830 to his death in 1865, he insisted that it was in Britain's interest that European regimes follow the British model of limited monarchy and parliamentary government. Once again, he was a man of contradictions. His critics saw him as an adventurer whose pursuit of liberal goals abroad were used to justify his gunboat diplomacy. He became notorious in some European capitals, and his dispatches triggered thoughts of mobilization and ships of war. If Lord Castlereagh's critical response to the advent of post-Napoleonic absolutism was splendid isolationism, Palmerston's was a form of diplomatic interventionism called brinksmanship by his critics. Whether he was meddling in Spanish royal marriage arrangements, risking war over an obscure shopkeeper named Don Pacifico, or coaxing England into a war in the distant Crimea, he elevated the nation's consciousness to its purposeful role in the world. Such conduct, it is thought, further destabilized a Europe already threatened with revolutionary nationalism, neo-Bonapartism and growing militarism.

On the other hand, revisionist historians have seen Palmerston as the architect of an international system who shrewdly met the nation's interests by controlling the tides of change taking place in Europe and America. After a long apprenticeship, he grew to understand the complex forces at work in a post-Napoleonic world and then mastered them in serving British interests first and foremost. It could then be argued that in pursuing those interests, the peace of Europe was secured and the cause of freedom advanced. Studying Palmerston's influence on foreign affairs entails tracing his actions from his early days at the Admiralty and the War Office (when his inclination towards assertive diplomacy first appeared) to when he truly placed his stamp on the Foreign Office in the 1830s. The standards he set for his staff, exemplified by his own tireless labours, and his purposefulness, left no doubt in diplomats' minds that he personally spoke for the nation in defining its foreign policy.

Understanding the guiding principles of straightforward, often abrasive Palmerstonianism means also reconciling it with his craven opportunism. In the case of France, he first praised Louis Philippe's constitutional monarchy only to risk destroying the *Entente Cordiale* by abandoning it in 1848. He supported Italian liberalism and nationalism yet turned an indifferent face to such movements in Poland. He made overtures to the Russian Tsar, only to go elsewhere for allies. Underneath this highly improvisational style lay a substantial commitment to the advancement of Britain's interests, defined in terms of the peaceful enjoyment of freedom and prosperity for its people. Such interests, however, could only be realized, according to Palmerston, if his country was unhampered by entangling alliances and free of ideological constraints.

Controversy has also surrounded Palmerston's contribution to the evolution of party politics in nineteenth-century Britain. It is a truism that modern political parties tend to become divided, leaderless and fall into disarray when they struggle to adapt their party principles to new issues in changing times. Central to how politicians responded to the crucial issues raised in the wake of the Industrial Revolution (such as the condition of the working classes, a sharpening of class conflict and demands for an expanded franchise) was the state of the political party system. Although sometimes seen as standing aloof from party politics, could a man who served in government for almost half a century not play a significant role in influencing the state of parties for the future? The traditional Whig and Tory parties had been weakened and divided over such issues as parliamentary reform, Catholic Emancipation, the New Poor Law and, most importantly, free trade. Disagreements among the Tories that originated in the Liverpool ministry and which then resurfaced in the split over free trade, produced two minority parties where there had been one. Similarly, despite the show of unity in 1832 with the passage of the Reform Bill, the Whigs (serially led by Lords Grey, Melbourne and John Russell) drifted into conservative camps. This picture of disintegration is not complete without adding an assortment of radicals of various shades and an Irish minority who rallied around Daniel O'Connell in their quest for the repeal of the Act of Union. Although government was not paralysed by indecision, by the late 1840s few cabinets formed with coherent programmes. By 1852, the best Queen Victoria could do was to have Lord Aberdeen construct a loosely tied coalition representing key parliamentary factions.

Meanwhile, in this state of political disunity, Palmerston was able to command centre stage by stealing the initiative to operate outside of, and above, party. This meant that, despite his loose affiliation with the Whigs and new radical connections, Palmerston operated as his own man. Increasingly, in both domestic and foreign affairs, he acted outside the halls of Parliament by appealing directly to the people. In doing so, Palmerston raised serious questions about the traditional party system and about parliament's role in public discourse. Did he replace parliamentary deliberation with the demagogic politics of the public platform? If so, what does this say about his ability to adapt his aristocratic principles to the demands of a democratic age and to meet the challenge of political transformation in a non-revolutionary way?

Allied to these questions, but deserving of special attention, is the fact that Palmerston led the way as unequalled interpreter of the national mood after the 1850s. In shifting the debate over the political agenda away from Parliament to a more public forum, he not only cultivated his own reputation as a man of the people, but also invited the public to have their own impact on government policy. The manner in which this was done provides a commentary on the power of the press acting as a liaison between an increasingly literate population and their leaders. It also shows how a single individual could exert his leadership by reaching out to diverse classes and interests and thereby uniting them around a self-confident understanding of what they stood for as a nation. In turn, the question is asked as to whether Palmerston had a conscious affinity with an audience of prosperous middle-class Victorians or, instead, merely manipulated the instincts and sentiments of an easily swayed and still immature public. All of these questions provide an opportunity to reflect on the broader issues of the state of British nationalism, how it was shaped, and its impact on the development of public policy.

If it can be shown that Palmerston did indeed become a master of public sentiment who captured and shaped British nationalism at the height of the Victorian age, then perhaps his place in modern British history will be established. No longer can he be simplistically characterized as an anachronism that had outlived his usefulness in a rapidly modernizing world. More accurately, he can be studied as a man of many parts, evolving politically and adapting constantly to meet the challenges of changing circumstances. In this sense, his life must be viewed not merely in terms of his aristocratic origins or as a brake upon progress but also as an individual who steadily helped to define his own time and provided a blueprint for the advancing democratic age.

1

THE MAKING OF A CANNINGITE

In 1806 Palmerston entered politics against a background of overarching events that would dominate his early public life and bring Britain to the cusp of greatness. Britain had already distinguished herself from other nations as a pioneer in the Industrial Revolution. With the French Revolution's ideological influence still shaping people's minds, the British had launched into the second phase of the Napoleonic wars. Although Napoleon's armies dominated the mainland of Europe, Horatio Nelson's victory over the Franco-Spanish fleet at Trafalgar in October 1805 meant that Britain would command the seas, thus precluding any French invasion across the Channel.

The political world that Palmerston entered in 1806 was in disarray. British political parties, torn apart by differences in their ranks, were struggling to realign themselves. The Whigs, divided after Edmund Burke's break with Charles James Fox over the French Revolution, had been left in the political wilderness until a group led by the Duke of Portland accepted William Pitt's invitation to form a coalition in 1794. Meanwhile, the Foxites, less fearful of Jacobinical influences in Britain than Portland, stayed out in the political cold.

Just as the French Revolution became a defining issue on which ministries rose or fell, the issue of relief for Irish Catholics and their political disabilities drove politicians into different camps. In believing that his constitutional oath prevented him from allowing Roman Catholics entry to government, George III opposed any change in policy. The King's intolerance of Catholic Emancipation drove Pitt from office in 1801 and helped to bring down Grenville's Ministry of All the Talents in 1807. On the other hand, 'Protestant' ministries such as those of

Spencer Percival in 1809 and Lord Liverpool in 1812 enjoyed greater favour at court. As the regency years proceeded, however, the Catholic Question drove a wedge between the staunchly Protestant ultra Tories and the newly emerging liberal Tories.

As these issues loomed large both at home and abroad in Palmerston's public life, could any contemporary observer have predicted that this callow twenty-one-year-old man would dominate his country in forty years? Born and bred an aristocrat, he would seem to have more of a vested interest in conserving the past than in looking to the future. However, all of that would change as he immersed himself in the workaday life of government service, and the lines of his political personality became discernible.

Given his family's Pittite ties, it was no surprise that Palmerston stood as a Tory for the parliamentary seat of Cambridge left vacant by Pitt's death in January 1806. Palmerston's rivals were the sons of Whig magnates: Lord Henry Petty, the son of the Marquess of Lansdowne, and Lord Althorp, son of Earl Spencer. Palmerston had counted on support from fellow 'Johnians' (those associated with his college, St John's) but it was not enough. Petty, Chancellor of the Exchequer in the new Grenville ministry, had patronage power at his disposal and won easily with 331 votes, while Althorp and Palmerston trailed with 145 and 128 votes, respectively.[1]

The key campaign issue had been the abolition of the slave trade. Support had grown for abolition since 1791 when William Wilberforce awakened consciences to the slave trade's cruelties. Thereafter, lines became drawn between those radicals and liberal Whigs who supported abolition and the conservative Whigs and Tories who opposed it, thinking it too Jacobinical. Petty favoured abolition but Palmerston, whose family had been linked with anti-abolitionism, found himself on the wrong side of the issue. It was presumed that since his father had opposed abolition his son would follow his lead. Similarly, since the Third Viscount's Tory friends had opposed abolition, it was thought that they spoke for him. The Whig reformer Henry Brougham went out of his way to characterize the younger Palmerston as an anti-reformer and the label stuck throughout the campaign. In fact, Palmerston's speeches are silent about the slave trade, although other contemporary issues were addressed. Although Parliament's abolition of the slave trade in 1807 dispensed with it as a political issue for Palmerston, he was eventually to become an outspoken advocate of abolition's enforcement as he became increasingly reform-minded.[2]

Other unsuccessful bids for parliamentary seats in Horsham and Cambridge followed in 1807. Because of his aristocratic connections, a seat was finally found for him in the pocket borough of Newport on the Isle of Wight, a constituency once represented by his father. Earlier in 1807, George III, annoyed by Grenville's renewed support for Catholic Emancipation, turned to the Duke of Portland to form a Tory government. The Tories' return to office brought with it the appointment of Palmerston as a junior lord of the Admiralty Board. Although this was a sinecure position – merely requiring the board members to sign their names to official documents – Palmerston seemed to make the most of this office. It exposed him to government operations and to numerous administrative reports. Although not challenged by his work, he had the opportunity to show others that he was an industrious and serious politician.[3] Palmerston finally took his seat in the House of Commons in June 1807 and stayed there until his death in 1865. Although he had an Irish peerage, it did not entitle him to a place in the British House of Lords. Years later he was offered a seat in the Lords, but preferred to exert his leadership in the Commons.

In contrast to his later pre-eminence in Parliament, Palmerston's early years were inauspicious. Predictably, he championed Pittite war policies and it was expected that he would support the twin pillars of the established church and the monarchy against attempts to repeal the Test Acts or embarrass George III with motions for Catholic Emancipation. His statements on the hustings, however, were uncontroversial and his maiden speech in Parliament did not come until February 1808. The speech itself was flawed with the usual mistakes of a beginner and to some he gave a poor impression.[4] Nevertheless, it provided an early indication of his thoughts on the Napoleonic War and foreign policy in general. By 1807, the war had turned badly against Britain. Nelson's victory at Trafalgar had been eclipsed by Napoleon's successive victories over Prussia in 1806 and Russia in 1807. The Berlin Decree of 1806 had closed all ports under French control to British shipping. This stranglehold on exports tightened when Napoleon dictated terms to Tsar Alexander at Tilsit in 1807. By this treaty, ports not already under French hegemony fell under Napoleon's shadow, including those in Sweden and Denmark. In the latter case, it was apparent from intelligence reports that the Danish fleet would soon fall to the French. At the urging of Canning, then Foreign Secretary, after demanding that the Danes surrender their fleet for the duration of the war, the British attacked Copenhagen.

The Whigs sharply criticized the Copenhagen expedition, with Lord Grey declaring that Britain had been embarrassed by this act of injustice. Palmerston used his maiden speech to echo Canning's remarks: he argued that British intervention in Denmark was required because Napoleon threatened to capture the Danish fleet. Although he recognized that international law should be observed, he felt that necessity dictated action be taken.[5]

While Palmerston's speech in 1808 was hardly a defining moment in the evolution of his political life, it clearly aligned him with the Portland ministry's war policy and placed him in the same camp as the belligerent Canning. Nevertheless, Palmerston's network of relationships in this new alignment kept shifting, as the men and measures that dominated an increasingly fragmented Portland administration changed. The Tories, already divided on the war issue by a faction led by Lord Sidmouth, were suffering from other divisions – Portland's poor health encouraged ambitious Tories to jockey for leadership positions, and a bitter rivalry between Viscount Castlereagh and Canning threatened to break up the ministry. As the War Office dragged its feet in executing a new offensive in Germany or Portugal, Canning, who preferred a forward policy on the continent, worked behind the scenes to dislodge Castlereagh. Fearful that the government would collapse, Portland agreed to make some changes but events moved too quickly to avoid a ministerial crisis.

In July 1809, the government embarked on its Peninsular War to drive the French out of Spain and Portugal. By the end of the month, Arthur Wellesley's victory at Talavera in Spain had turned the tide against Napoleon and in the process he earned himself the title of the Duke of Wellington. Another offensive with less happy results was launched up the Scheldt River, aimed at destroying the docks and fleet in Antwerp. This campaign, muted by Austria's capitulation to the French at Wagram in July, turned into a disaster. The decision to abandon the Copenhagen campaign, leaving fever-ridden troops behind on Walcheren Island, was a humiliation that the government could not survive. Meanwhile, the dispute between Canning and Castlereagh was exposed to public view as the former used the Walcheren débâcle to undermine his rival's standing. The two survived a duel in September but lost their positions in the government. With their resignations and Portland's death later in the year, the king turned to Spencer Percival, the Tory evangelical, to refashion the Cabinet.

Likely candidates for Percival's new Cabinet were not easy to find. Canning and Castlereagh's resignations made them unavailable while persistent differences on the war issue kept other Tories apart. Although Percival made overtures to the Whigs, the response was lukewarm. The best he could hope for was a reprise of the Ministry of All the Talents. George III demanded that the Catholic Question should not be treated as an open question as a condition for appointment. Moreover, given Percival's access to the royal ear, the Whigs could see that they would be relegated to the role of junior partners in a coalition government. The failure to form a government of leading men meant the formation of a ministry of lesser talents. Denied such experienced hands as Canning and Castlereagh, Percival made uninspired choices.

It was against this background that Percival offered Palmerston the position of Chancellor of the Exchequer in October 1809. That this twenty-four-year-old junior Lord of the Admiralty, known more for the mark he was making in high society than in politics, should be considered for this highly responsible office was more a reflection of the dearth of talent available than of Palmerston's ascendancy in the Tory party. Although Palmerston may have assumed that some place would be found for him in the new ministry, the offer of the Exchequer came as a surprise.[6] As someone with no experience in finance and no record of accomplishment in Parliament, he was miscast for the role. Palmerston knew that he was considered second best for he was told that others had already refused the office.[7] Surprisingly, Palmerston turned down the offer and accepted instead the lesser position of Secretary at War. His reasoning reveals something about his political realism at this time as well as his hopes for the future. As he was so inexperienced, he foresaw that he would be an easy target for the Opposition. While still suffering from the humiliation of Walcheren, the Chancellor of the Exchequer, Palmerston thought, would be vulnerable to Whig sniping. Lacking the parliamentary skills of a Pitt or Fox, he feared that his inability to respond to these attacks would lead to the collapse of the ministry.[8]

Much has been made of Palmerston's failure to seize this opportunity to vault ahead in politics. Those who know the later Palmerston for his self-confident assertiveness would find this younger man uncharacteristically self-effacing. Moreover, in choosing the War Office he seemed to trap himself in a dead-end administrative post where he remained for nineteen years. It also could be said that in rejecting the Exchequer he missed the opportunity to project himself forward as an alternative to Castlereagh or Canning. Understandably, Palmerston's biographers see this missed opportunity as a turning-point in his early career.

Most agree that he lacked confidence and feared that if he were too ambitious, his reach would exceed his grasp. Anyone who places himself too high, he told Malmesbury at this time, 'rises to fall the lower'.[9] In turning down the Exchequer for the War Office, Herbert Bell suggests that he was acting more out of practical shrewdness than out of modesty. The War Office provided a novice politician with an opportunity to learn while enhancing his reputation.[10] Donald Southgate says that Palmerston's caution was due to his hard-headed calculation that he would be risking his future if he were unprepared for the work ahead of him. Kenneth Bourne, on the other hand, suggests that Palmerston was also concerned about the state of the nation in 1809. According to him, given the public uproar over the Walcheren disaster, the low ebb of British fortunes in the war, and the Percival ministry's vulnerability, Palmerston realized that it would be untimely for him to accept this office.[11]

Being in the War Office for the next nineteen years did not mean that Palmerston had found a safe harbour from the storms of political controversy. As Secretary at War, his position was circumscribed by the roles played by others. For example, the more senior minister (the Secretary of War and the Colonies) was responsible for establishing the policy and the direction of war. He did not run the day-to-day operations of the War Office. It fell to the Commander-in-Chief to deal with strictly military functions as well as personnel and disciplinary matters. Normally, this officer would be a royal duke who operated outside of the War Office at the Horse Guards. The Commander-in-Chief also acted as a liaison between the crown and the army and was answerable only to the king. Other militarily related functions also lay outside the purview of the Secretary at War. For example, the issue of arms, equipment, ammunition and other supplies came from the Board of Ordnance and the Commissary-General, whereas the Treasury, acting through the Paymaster-General, paid the army. However, the Secretary at War, working as an intermediary between Parliament and the army, addressed financial and other issues that overlapped the jurisdiction of several military departments and especially that of the Commander-in-Chief.

At the heart of this confusion of roles was a constitutional issue similar to the one fought between George III and the encroaching powers of Parliament. As Secretary at War, Palmerston was caught in crossfire. He was in the unenviable position of having to defend the government's management of the army to the House of Commons while at the same time acting as Parliament's agent in curtailing military abuses. These inter-office tensions had predated Palmerston's arrival at the War Office but were reawakened by a renewed effort to reform widespread army abuses. Many of these abuses were attributable to the War Office's tolerance of ill-disciplined employees who were under-worked and over-paid.[12] Over the years, various recommendations had been made to reform the system and to increase the number of trained personnel. In addition, various proposals had been made to centralize the process of managing regimental accounts. However, although defenders of the status quo (such as the Commander-in-Chief) resisted such reforms during wartime, their jurisdictional authority was now being questioned in what promised to be a major inter-office conflict.

Although he did not have a reputation as a reformer, Palmerston was ready to implement reforms when he came to the War Office. In particular, he relished taking on the entrenched interests at the Horse Guards represented by General Sir David Dundas, a 74-year-old veteran who boasted of climbing to high rank from humble origins. Dundas predictably reacted fiercely to the War Office reforms by demanding that his office not be circumvented.[13] Palmerston had already had a run-in with Dundas when he rejected a warrant giving a sinecure position at the Chelsea Hospital to Lt General Oliver De Lancey, an in-law of Dundas. De Lancey had gained a reputation for skimming public funds when he had been Barracks-Master General, and his case was furthered damaged when it was later discovered that he was in charge of non-existent barracks.[14] Percival supported Palmerston and the appointment was denied. This was one in a series of rows between the War Office and the Horse Guards that was symptomatic of a deeper underlying problem. At issue was whether the Secretary at War was subordinate to the Commander-in-Chief or whether he enjoyed the freedom to speak for the civilian branch of the government.[15] Dundas's resignation in May 1811 did not ease Palmerston's relationship with the Horse Guards. The jurisdictional conflict persisted when successive Commanders-in-Chief, such as the Dukes of York and Wellington, challenged Palmerston's duty to report the army estimates to Parliament.[16]

Unlike his faltering performance in Parliament in 1808, Palmerston was seen as a thoroughly competent government spokesman in the House of Commons.[17] He was fortunate because as the war intensified on the continent, the Opposition was reluctant to speak against increased expenditures. After Waterloo, the Opposition, led mainly by the stubborn Scottish radical Joseph Hume, thought only in terms of a peacetime military budget. In making his relentless attacks upon the army estimates, Hume demanded that the War Office return to the 1792 peacetime budget. Palmerston stood his ground, arguing that the 1815 Vienna settlement made it impossible for Britain to abandon her new responsibilities around the globe. Moreover, he said that unrest and violence, as seen in the Luddite riots, required military readiness at home.[18]

By following this line of reasoning, Palmerston associated himself with the government's repressive policy against rioters and agitators in the period after 1812. He had already become the target of the radicals when he defended the use of flogging as a disciplinary measure in the army.[19] Postwar repression continued in the wake of the Spa Field riots of 1816, when the government barred public meetings attended by 50 or more people, curtailed freedom of the press, and suspended the Habeas Corpus Act. Palmerston also responded harshly to the tumultuous events of 1819. As Secretary at War, he championed order at the expense of certain freedoms. When troops fired on people gathered at St Peter's Field in Manchester in 1819, he unhesitatingly defended the soldiers' action. Similarly, Palmerston joined other ministers in saying that Lord Sidmouth's infamous Six Acts of 1819 had not gone far enough in curtailing freedom of the press. These were strange words coming from a man who later depended on newspapers to broadcast his views to the nation. Whether he sought larger standing armies or sought to quarter troops in barracks so as to isolate them from the rowdy public, Palmerston was characterized by his critics as an enemy of freeborn Englishmen.[20] To all appearances, Palmerston looked like a typical Tory enforcing the will of a government unable to address imaginatively the social discontents of the day.

Palmerston could also be relied upon to support the government when new challenges faced the Liverpool ministry in 1820. The year began with the death of the long-ailing George III on 29 January. Beleaguered by criticism over the state of the country, the Tories gained some reassurance in February with a comfortable victory in the parliamentary general election against an even weaker Whig party. In the same month, the Cato Street conspiracy to assassinate ministers was uncovered, suggesting that plots and insurrections still bedevilled the nation. Then word came from abroad that the new king's wife, the estranged Queen Caroline – whose name had already been sullied by charges of adultery – was returning to England to claim her place on the throne. After initial attempts at bribing the Queen to stay on the Continent had failed, George IV sought a bill of divorce. When the Queen was received warmly upon her arrival in England on 5 June, it was not easy for the government to abandon her when the parliamentary Opposition had already caught the mood of the crowd. Clearly, the people outdoors were recoiling against a king, who despite his own moral laxity was seen as hypocritically turning on his wife.

As the Queen's popularity grew in 1820 and then intensified at the news of her death in the summer of 1821, Palmerston found himself in the unenviable position of speaking for the government. He was directly drawn into the controversy when, speaking in his capacity as Secretary at War, he defended the King's recent dismissal of General Sir Robert Wilson, a distinguished veteran of the Peninsular and Russian campaigns, who had become a radical spokesman for popular causes. Wilson had been dismissed from the army when he stopped troops from attacking a noisy crowd following Queen Caroline's funeral procession. Against a volley of Opposition criticism, Palmerston asserted that Wilson had failed to do his duty in disciplining an unruly mob, thereby endangering the lives of others.[21] Once again, Palmerston found himself acting as the government's mouthpiece in repeating the Tory law and order message.

Thus far, there was little evidence in Palmerston's career to distinguish him from other Tory office-holders. Although offered other government positions, he resigned himself to the War Office. He could have become Chief Secretary for Ireland or Governor-General of India but he refused without hesitation as these offers were lateral moves and provided little opportunity for advancement.[22] Nor did an invitation to become Postmaster-General along with being named an English peer tempt Palmerston. Other Irish peers might consider it an elevation in rank to move to the House of Lords, but Palmerston, warming to the interplay of debate in the House of Commons, chose to keep his seat.[23]

Palmerston's seeming disinterest in positions outside of the War Office and especially foreign assignments may be in part attributable to his active social calendar in London and at his Broadlands estate. Suppers, dances and the theatre preoccupied his evening hours in the social whirl of the *beau monde*. As a very eligible bachelor, it did not take long for him to gain entry to the private clubs patronized by such notables as Lady Jersey, the Whig socialite known for her important connections. He quickly earned a reputation as a womanizer and cultivated close, if not intimate, ties with such celebrities as Princess Lieven, wife of the Russian ambassador and mistress to a galaxy of statesmen, including Metternich and Guizot. But if Palmerston's gaze fell on anyone, it was Emily Lamb, the wife of Earl Cowper and sister of the second Viscount Melbourne. Familiar with her family since childhood, Palmerston began a flirtation in 1809 that blossomed into a long-term affair, leading to their marriage in 1839. This relationship, rumoured to have produced some of Lady Cowper's children, was a matter of public record, which seems to enhance rather than mar Palmerston's reputation. It was these women, acting as the patronesses of such clubs as Almack's, who provided Palmerston with the back channels to the latest political gossip. Although these well-developed connections or amorous ties did not harm his reputation, they did not seem to advance him politically. He was not seen as a rising star among the Tories nor had he cultivated new relationships with the Whigs. Now reaching his late thirties, he seemed complacently satisfied with his career, with few prospects for political advancement.[24]

However, the year 1822 was to signal changes in Tory politics that were bound to affect Palmerston's future. On 12 August 1822, Viscount Castlereagh, overwhelmed with work as Foreign Secretary and leader of the government in the House of Commons, committed suicide. In what has been called a cataclysmic event, the Tory party was transformed.[25] Already suffering from breaks in its ranks, Castlereagh's death – and his replacement at the Foreign Office by Canning – exposed the ministry's divisions to full public view. Canning had already become a lightning rod for controversy and disagreement. Other Tories looked down on Canning due to his questionable origins as the son of an actress. Nor did it help his standing at court when his support for Queen Caroline in 1820 outraged George IV, making his prospects for future advancement bleak. However, Castlereagh's suicide was to change all of that. Although Lord Liverpool, Prime Minister since 1812, turned to Robert Peel to take the lead in the House of Commons, Canning seemed to be the inevitable choice for the Foreign Office.[26]

With Canning's ascent to the Foreign Office came some important ministerial shifts in style, if not substance. In general, both Castlereagh and Canning had distanced themselves from the other Concert Powers, namely illiberal Austria, Russia, Prussia and France. In his State Paper of 5 May 1820, Castlereagh had repudiated forceful intervention by one state in the affairs of another. While any talk that threatened the break-up of the Concert worried Castlereagh, Canning saw it as an opportunity for Britain to challenge the aggressive designs of nations such as France or Russia. The occasion for a dramatic redefinition of British foreign policy came in 1822 at the Congress of Verona where the Concert Powers supported French intervention in Spain to assist Ferdinand VII's rejection of the 1812 liberal constitution. In 1820, liberal insurgents had forced Ferdinand VII to recognize the constitution originally fostered by Napoleon. Faced with the challenge of a French invasion of Spain, Canning scolded France and warned that future acts of repression would not be tolerated. Then, in 1823, he did not hesitate to use troops to keep Ferdinand from overthrowing the constitutional monarchy of Queen Maria of Portugal.[27] One year later, in protecting the newly liberated South American colonies from interference by European states, Canning set forth the seminal warning later echoed in the Monroe Doctrine.[28]

These dramatic reformulations of British foreign policy had their own political impact on the fragile condition of the Liverpool ministry. Some ministers, especially Wellington, saw Canning's defence of the new South American republics as a spur to revolutionary movements in Europe. For his part, Canning considered his action as consistent with British parliamentarianism, as well as an opportunity to convert spheres of Spanish colonialism into enterprise zones for British trade. Other differences also undermined the ministry's unity. Although Canning had never been a friend to liberal causes at home, he did break ranks with the ultra-Tories over Catholic Emancipation. Next to their staunch defence of the monarchy, opposition to Catholic Emancipation had been a defining issue that distinguished Tories from Whigs at the end George III' s reign. As liberal causes were advanced in Europe and America, it was not difficult for ultra-Tory ministers to make connections with the threat of revolution being fomented in Ireland. If Simon Bolivar could win independence for states in South America, could Daniel O'Connell's demand for Catholic representation in Parliament lead eventually to Irish self-rule? As O'Connell's highly successful Catholic Association, founded in 1823, continued to galvanize support for Catholic Emancipation, it was difficult for the Tories to avoid this issue as they had done in the past. Before that happened, however, the ministers had to face up to their own differences which risked the possibility of driving them further apart and exposing their fractured condition.

Prior to this, Palmerston's duties at the War Office had not drawn him into the Cabinet debate and he was not inclined to attach himself to any renegade movement. A Canningite wing of the party had begun to emerge, but Palmerston had not been aligned with it. He and Canning had little in common, but there is no evidence of any obstacle that separated them. As new issues emerged after 1822 that forced the Tories to divide along either progressive or conservative lines, Palmerston and Canning and other like-minded politicians began to act as a unit. The one issue that separated Palmerston from conservative or ultra-Tories was Catholic Emancipation. As an Irish Protestant landlord, he was a committed supporter of the established church, but he had consistently been sympathetic to the plight of his Irish Catholic tenants and their political disabilities. As a young landlord, he had fostered improvements on his Sligo estates, including the establishment of schools for peasant children. Moreover, he had persistently tried to reclaim the land in Sligo for the sake of better agricultural productivity while also improving the harbour with hopes of developing local fishing resources.[29]

Beyond his personal sympathy for the plight of Irish Catholics, Palmerston's espousal of Catholic Emancipation was a process of slow growth based less on religious conviction and abstract theory and more on practical expediency. He had treated the issue rather gingerly in his ill-fated run for Cambridge in 1807, knowing that there was an anti-papal mood in the university.[30] However, by 1813 (although he now sat for Cambridge and was returned there in 1818 and 1820) he felt free to speak his mind openly. Recognizing that Catholic representation in Parliament was inevitable, he said, 'It is vain to think that by any human pressure we can stop the spring which gushes from the earth.' He further argued that as a practical matter, the nation needed the Catholics' services, and repression would only drive them underground.[31] Palmerston knew that by taking this position he had put himself at odds with his fellow ministers, but he hoped that he could treat Catholic Emancipation as an open question.

The Catholic Question was not an issue that he could easily avoid in his Cambridge constituency. He was advised by some of his friends to vote for a change but not to speak out in the Commons.[32] By 1825, Palmerston had lost whatever inhibitions he had had to speak out on the subject. When Sir Francis Burdett introduced Catholic Emancipation in February 1825, he voted with the majority of 21. Burdett's motion was later rejected in the Lords, but the Cabinet could not keep it out of the public eye.[33] It was obvious that this issue, despite Liverpool's desire to play down its significance, had to be addressed in the forthcoming 1826 parliamentary elections. Indeed, it has been argued that the Duke of Wellington had urged Liverpool to call a general election, hoping to profit from anti-Catholic sentiment aroused by the recent debate.[34]

Palmerston's vote on the Burdett motion had clearly positioned him with the 'Catholics' in the Liverpool administration, leaving him open to attacks from the High Tories. If this growing breach was not already evident, it became clear when Palmerston fought to keep his seat at Cambridge in 1826. Since all three of his opponents were 'Protestants', he assumed that they would split the Tory vote, while he would attract liberal Tory and Whig support.[35] In the end, Henry Bankes, his old associate in the government, polled 508 votes while Henry Goulborn, the Secretary for Ireland received 437 votes. John Copley, the Attorney General, headed the poll with 772 ballots, but Palmerston's 631 was enough to win the second seat.[36]

Despite his victory, it was difficult for Palmerston to accept easily the ultra-Tory attack against him by Lords Eldon and Bathurst. He believed that the ultras' betrayal of him in the 1826 election would be seen as an open breach amounting to an abandonment of Pittite orthodoxy. He insisted, for example, that unlike the ultras, he had remained faithful to William Pitt's principles, especially support for Catholic Emancipation and lower taxes on grain.[37] Also, his long-standing dispute with the Duke of York over the latter's role as Commander-in-Chief had soured his relationship with those at court, and his inclination to favour the gradual abolition of colonial slavery separated him from the High Tories. He had been a consistent supporter of the Anti-Slavery Society since 1820, and in 1826 he brought a petition from his Cambridge constituents seeking gradual abolition, arguing that it was entirely consistent with Cambridge University's commitment to Christian principles.[38]

As the year 1826 ended it was apparent that there were more issues dividing the Tories than uniting them. This division widened when Canning's ally on the Board of Trade, William Huskisson, moved to revise the Corn Laws to the consternation of Tory landlord interests. With as many Whigs aligned with liberal Tories as there were ultra-Tories speaking in Opposition, party allegiances blurred. Palmerston did not take an active part in the Corn Law debates but it is clear that he was inclined to support Huskisson's liberal commercial policy.[39]

Palmerston's place in the hurly-burly of party politics became clearer by 1827. Thus far, his emergence as a loyal Canningite had done nothing to change his status as a minor politician. However, the situation started to change with the death of his nemesis, the Duke of York. The Duke's death not only silenced a loud Protestant voice, but it also cleared the way for the less intransigent Duke of Clarence to succeed to the throne on the death of the childless George IV in 1830. For Palmerston this meant that he had one less competitor at the War Office, but it hardly signalled any major improvement in his status. However, Liverpool's sudden death on 17 February 1827 changed Palmerston's fortunes dramatically. Liverpool had been the glue that kept the fragile Tory Cabinet together, and his departure made Canning his likely successor, with places for his followers. It was also clear that Canning's positions on foreign policy, the Corn Laws and the Catholic Question were incompatible with the views of men like Peel and Wellington. Overtures for office had already been put out to the Whigs and, after prolonged negotiations, a Tory–Whig coalition was formed in April 1827.[40] This reshuffle of the Cabinet permitted Canning's loyalists, principally William Huskisson, Lord Dudley, Charles Grant and Palmerston, to join him. While Palmerston's commitment to Canning was beyond question at this point, it is uncertain whether the feelings were mutual. On 14 April, Canning offered Palmerston the Exchequer with a seat in the Cabinet but then withdrew it on 10 June after months of further negotiation.[41] Ostensibly, the offer was withdrawn when Canning lamely argued that the burden of standing for a coming by-election would prevent Palmerston from undertaking duties at the Exchequer. Instead, it was suggested that the appointment to the Exchequer be postponed until later in the session when time permitted Palmerston to visit his Cambridge constituents.

Other reasons help explain Canning's change of heart. For example, George IV's disdain for Palmerston persisted and apparently Canning himself did not have a very high estimate of his abilities. That certainly was the view of *The Times*, whose editors scoffed at the idea that Palmerston was worthy of the position. There was also some speculation that, like his father, he had mismanaged his personal finances. Palmerston's name had been linked with an investment scandal as a Director of the Devon and Cornwall Mining Company. Although Palmerston claimed that he had been only remotely involved with the company and had enjoyed no profit from his investment, the attacks persisted.[42] Offers to become Governor-General of Jamaica and India were made, but such consolation prizes were not appealing to Palmerston. Instead, he retreated to the War Office, but with the added advantage of being elevated to the Cabinet.[43]

While this is only a minor episode in the larger story of a Tory party in flux, it provides further commentary on Palmerston's status as a politician. Clearly, he was not yet a major player on the political stage and was not taken seriously for key positions. Still, now that he had access to Cabinet reports, he could address a variety of issues with greater authority. A further sign of his increasing influence was seen in the appointment of his brother, William Temple, first as Secretary of the Russian Embassy and then as *chargé d'affaires* in St Petersburg. This was no mere sinecure office and, as seen in the active correspondence between the two brothers, the position was to prove a very useful channel of information for Palmerston as he became more involved in the Eastern Question.[44]

Sickness and death continued to shape events in August 1827 when Canning died at the age of 57. Although not unexpected, his death left a leadership void in the government, leaving George IV with few alternatives. He was averse to having a Whig Prime Minister and knew that restoring either Peel or Wellington to office would mean the return of Tory factionalism. In desperation, he chose the inept and indecisive Frederick Robinson, now Lord Goderich. Goderich was faced with the unenviable task of either forming a government made up of ultra-Tories estranged from Canningites or relying on Whigs displeasing to the King.[45] In the political manoeuvring that followed, it was apparent that the Canningites and their leader's principles had survived. Huskisson, Grant, Dudley and Palmerston held their places in the Cabinet but talk of change was in the air. In August there was renewed speculation about Palmerston going to the Exchequer, but this was thwarted by the King's desire to nominate John Herries, a protectionist Tory and 'Protestant' for that position. In the end, lacking sufficient Whigs or ultra-Tories, Goderich created a hodge-podge body unidentifiable with any party. The Canningites retained their places, with Huskisson emerging as the leader in the Commons. This did not suffice to hold these quarrelsome ministers together. In frustration, the ineffectual Goderich resigned in January 1828, forcing the King to turn to Wellington to form a new government.

Realizing that he could not construct a 'Protestant Cabinet', the best that George IV could do was to resurrect the remnants of the Liverpool ministry. This meant restoring a select number of conservative Tories, as well as Canningites who would exact a price for their cooperation. In discussions with the Canningites at Apsley House, Wellington agreed to leave the Catholic Question open although the government would assume a neutral stance.[46] Huskisson's liberal commercial policy was adopted and support for Greek independence was reaffirmed, despite Wellington's misgivings about interventionism in the Near East.[47] This final condition would come back to haunt Wellington as foreign policy clashes, in which Palmerston was a feisty participant, continued to plague his Cabinet meetings.

The Apsley House agreement reveals as much about Palmerston's political evolution as it does about the state of the Tory party. Commenting privately, he exulted in what he saw as a victory over the ultra-Tories. More interesting still was his unequivocal recognition that he was a Canningite. 'But still we, the Canningites, if we may be so termed, did not join their Government, but they came and joined ours,' he said. If this show of his Canningite colours was not enough, he then went on to stipulate explicitly who was a true Canningite. While defending the need for a powerful landed aristocracy, he distinguished Canningites from ultras as men who were open to a limited extension of the suffrage, free trade, the end to religious disabilities and the advancement of constitutionalism abroad.[48] This defining statement, however, must be viewed circumspectly. The Canningites were at most a small group of friends who were willing to act together in advancing certain principles. They were not a party and they did not identify themselves with the Whigs. For Palmerston, however, it appears that after twenty years in public life he had reached a new level of political maturity. He was no longer simply the child of aristocratic privilege predictably tied to a Tory agenda. Clearly, he had come into his own as an outspoken, experienced politician who knew his own mind on the issues of the day. Although still rooted in his aristocratic values, twenty years in government had moved him to focus on persistent problems and to seek practical solutions.

As Palmerston foresaw in January, the Apsley House agreement turned out to be more of a challenge and an obstacle to Wellington than a commitment to ministerial cooperation. There were persistent differences over Huskisson's modification of the Corn Laws. Charles Grant, the Canningite at the Board of Trade, was so annoyed with Wellington's defence of protectionism that he quit the ministry, only to return at Palmerston's urging.[49] Palmerston, now emerging as a guiding force among the Canningites, showed no hesitation in pushing Wellington to make greater concessions to liberal proposals, but he also realized that to effect change he and his allies had to stay in office. If Grant had resigned over the Corn Laws then Huskisson would be pressed to do likewise. If that happened, then the remaining Canningites, surrounded by ultra-Tories, would be forced to leave office.

The Canningites stayed on, but not for long. In April 1828, when Russia, acting as protector of Greek independence, attacked the Turks, the Wellington ministry reacted equivocally. The Prime Minister counselled caution, especially in giving Russia free rein as a patron of the Greeks, but Palmerston and the Foreign Secretary, Lord Dudley, held up the Hellenic banner for Greece's outright independence from Turkey.[50] These differences might have destroyed the ministry but, instead, it was an unforeseen event that did so. In May, the ministers advanced a bill to disenfranchise the depopulated boroughs of Penrhyn and East Retford. There was general agreement that these boroughs should lose their two seats in the House. A disagreement over where these seats should be relocated arose, but a compromise was reached whereby East Retford went to the populous city of Birmingham while Penryhn went to a nearby hundred to appease the agriculturist interests. Then, without any notice, the ultras reneged by transferring the seat meant for Birmingham to the hundred of Bassetlaw. Palmerston opposed such a manoeuvre and was able to persuade Huskisson to stay with him when the House divided.[51] What followed had consequences that went far beyond this seemingly minor proceeding.

For the first time, this debate gave Palmerston the opportunity to define his views on Parliamentary reform. Like Canning, he was not a champion of wholesale reform. In fact, he carefully explained that he favoured granting representation to large cities where the franchise was blatantly lacking as a moderate alternative to sweeping reforms in the system. True to his aristocratic background, Palmerston feared revolutionary change, but understood that selective reform was a necessary response to the people's grievances.[52]

More immediately significant was the impact of Huskisson's vote on the fate of the Wellington ministry. When Wellington labelled the action of the Canningites as 'mutiny',[53] Huskisson resigned and his friends followed him into the Opposition. For the first time, Palmerston sat on the Opposition benches facing a solidly conservative Tory ministry. He had been reluctant to leave office, hoping to keep Canning's policies in play. Considering himself unmuzzled, he now spoke more forcefully for such causes as Catholic Emancipation and Britain's support for constitutional governments abroad. The Catholic question was re-ignited in the summer of 1828 when the head of the New Catholic Association, Daniel O'Connell, won the parliamentary seat for Country Clare. The Wellington ministry now faced the dilemma of denying O'Connell his seat in Parliament, which risked fomenting a civil war in Ireland, or estranging the ultra-Tories. The Ultras, already disturbed by the repeal of the Test and Corporation Acts in 1828, feared that Catholic Emancipation would empower the Irish Catholic majority while destroying the Protestant ascendancy. Despite the ultra-Tories' outcry, Wellington and Peel reluctantly shifted their support to emancipation and the bill was passed in April 1829. The King, fighting to save his Protestant constitution, thought of replacing Wellington with the Duke of Richmond, but this was not a realistic alternative.[54]

From the outset, Palmerston gave repeal his full backing. Following the logic used in his discussion of parliamentary reform, he argued that the nation must reform to prevent revolution. Toleration, he said, could be the only response to the threat of civil war and wholesale bloodletting in Ireland. Palmerston was not indifferent to the spectre of violence but, in recognizing that O'Connell's Catholic Association had become a model of legal protest, he pragmatically realized that the Irish cause was irrepressible, saying, 'Put down the Association? They might as well talk of putting down the winds of Heaven, or of chaining the ceaseless tides of the ocean.'[55] As a benevolent Irish Protestant landlord, seeking peace and stability in Ireland, and unmotivated by any abstract humanitarian principles, Palmerston simply called for a practical solution to a problem affecting the kingdom as a whole.

Although he continued to join the Opposition throughout 1829 and 1830 in supporting reform measures, he preoccupied himself on the floor of the House with foreign affairs. Beginning on 1 June 1829, in forceful speeches so unlike his past stumbling utterances, Palmerston began to articulate those doctrines that would characterize his thinking for decades to come. Alarmed at the coup staged in 1828 by Dom Miguel, the conservative uncle of Queen Maria of Portugal, he roundly accused Wellington of abandoning that country's movement toward constitutionalism and parliamentary government. As he spoke, several sub-themes emerged. Exceeding even Canning's rhetoric, he advanced the principle later to re-appear in the Don Pacifico Affair, that it was in the nation's best interest to intervene against foreign tyrants to protect the rights of British subjects and to promote liberty and civilization in general. Sketching in broad strokes, a foreign policy blueprint emerged that defined Britain's relationship with Europe and the world for the next thirty-five years.[56]

Central to Palmerston's vision of world politics was the issue of non-intervention in the internal affairs of sovereign states. Like Castlereagh and Canning before him, he feared that, by using the mechanism of the Concert of Europe, states like France and Russia could advance their own interests by assisting despots in suppressing constitutional movements. Such acts of intervention, he believed, threatened the balance of power and were contrary to Britain's interest in fostering the development of liberal regimes. Castlereagh and Canning had championed non-interventionism to protect the rights of independent states; now Palmerston carried that policy a step further by turning it on its head. When Dom Miguel threatened to replace Queen Maria's liberal government in Portugal with absolutism, Palmerston thought it appropriate for Britain to 'intermeddle', at least with words if not by force, to safeguard British interests. It was not enough for the Wellington government to assume a neutral stance towards Dom Miguel's interference in Portugal, and Palmerston called for action if only verbal in nature. While finding its roots in Canningite boldness, this pronouncement was a new departure prefiguring the Palmerstonian adventurism to come.[57]

Meanwhile, the Wellington ministry, damaged seriously if not fatally by the vote on Catholic Emancipation, was foundering. Curiously, it had gained some temporary adherents among Whigs and radicals who had been pleased by Wellington and Peel's concession to the Catholics. However, poor harvests, driving up bread prices, and a decline in trade, causing severe unemployment, brought cries for currency and corn law revisions and, most of all, parliamentary reforms. By 1830, the combined effects of George IV's death in June and the news of the revolutions in France and Belgium increased the pressure for change.

In the wake of all these events, Wellington began seeking new blood for his Cabinet. Despite Palmerston's differences with Wellington, he was approached in early October 1829 about becoming the leader of the House of Commons in a ministry dominated by conservative Tories. If Palmerston joined such a Cabinet, he would have to do so without the free-trader Huskisson. Palmerston's reply to this highly speculative approach from the ultras amounted to a refusal. Although he had not discussed his views on free trade very often, he would not join a government that intended to reverse Huskisson's commercial reform achievements. Later, upon reflection, Palmerston was struck by the ultras' lack of realism in trying to mix 'Old fellows, saturated with the brine of Toryism, a few young men of the liberal parties, who shall not be able to set up as objections to any course proposed.... That they cannot agree, because it would be inconsistent with their own former pledges.' He concluded that, 'The Probability [*sic*] is that all will end in smoke & nothing be attempted before Parliament meets.'[58]

The year 1830 also witnessed a major shift in the political centre of gravity after almost a half-century of largely Tory rule. On 26 June, after months of failing health, George IV's death triggered significant train of events. Wellington now had to risk turning to a restive electorate in a general election. Also, the King's death brought his dim but affable brother, the Duke of Clarence, to the throne as William IV. Unlike the angry and obsessively anti-Whig George IV, the new king was not seen as an obstacle to a future Grey ministry. In the days preceding the general election there was growing evidence that the Whigs and the Huskissonians were drawing together. Although no union between the parties had been made, there was increasing talk about joining in systematic opposition.[59]

The election following the dissolution of Parliament on 24 July brought little change to the make-up of the House of Commons. There was a good deal of uncertainty about how new members might vote or how old members might shift their allegiance. It has been noted, however, that key contests went against the government and that Opposition candidates fared better especially in the more heavily populated constituencies. On the face of it, it appeared that Wellington's government still had the support of 250 members, in contrast to roughly 196 Opposition supporters and 212 uncommitted members.[60] Numbers aside, though, it seemed evident that there was a mood in the country for reform.

At this point, however, death intervened again to alter the political scene. In September, a locomotive at the opening of the Liverpool–Manchester railway line killed William Huskisson. With Huskisson gone, the chance that his followers would reach an understanding with the ministers faded, but not so with the Whigs. Men of talent and experience like Palmerston, Charles Grant and Lord Melbourne were attractive to the Whigs and could be relied upon to stand with them on various issues.

Before such an alliance could be formed in opposition to the ministry, Wellington committed a self-destructive act. In a parliamentary speech delivered on 2 November, he declared that his government had the people's confidence and therefore he was not compelled to propose a parliamentary reform bill.[61] However, not only had he miscalculated the country's mood, but by intransigently positioning himself on the right – perhaps in hopes of reclaiming some ultra-Tory support – Wellington doomed any eleventh hour rapprochement with the Canningites. Overtures were still being made to Palmerston at this late date, but when he told Wellington's emissary, Sir John Croker, that he was resolved to vote for parliamentary reform, negotiations ended abruptly.[62]

The Opposition's rejection of the Civil List on 15 November effectively forced the Wellington ministry to resign and Lord Grey to form a Whig ministry one day later. As this process went on, conversations had begun about Palmerston's role in the new government. Using the good offices of Lord Melbourne, an effort was made to advance Palmerston's name. There were fleeting references to his going to the Exchequer as well as leading the House of Commons, but serious talk centred on the Foreign Office. The meddlesome Princess Lieven flattered herself that it was her lobbying efforts with Grey that finally secured this place for Palmerston. Understandably, she preferred him for he was considered friendlier to Russia than Wellington had been, and she thought it would be reassuring to the regime in St Petersburg to have Palmerston's moderating influence on liberal Whigs.[63]

A better explanation for Palmerston's ascent to the Foreign Office can be found in his long apprenticeship toiling in the corridors of government, gradually insinuating himself into the political and social life of his day. More to the point, for the past few years he had been redefining himself as a Canningite and began carving a niche for himself in the area of foreign affairs. The first qualification allowed him to participate, although hesitantly, in the coming reform era, while the second made him eminently attractive to Lord Grey as someone who was sympathetic to the cause of constitutionalism advanced by the Whigs in foreign affairs. By championing liberal regimes abroad in his 1 June 1829 speech, Palmerston had demonstrated that he and the Whigs were like-minded. But it was in no way a foregone conclusion that he would go to the Foreign Office, for both Lansdowne and Holland had already been considered for the post.[64] It is noteworthy, however, that both men coupled their refusals of the office with the suggestion that Grey turn to Palmerston.

It was not that Palmerston had become a Whig so much as he was not the same Tory who had taken office in 1807. It is even doubtful that he would have been appealing to the Whigs in the early 1820s. In the intervening years he had proven himself to be a pragmatic politician open to liberal reforms. It would be an exaggeration to say that his conversion to liberalism was complete. Rather, he found himself hesitantly favouring reform as a way of avoiding revolution. Not surprisingly then, on 22 November 1830, when the new Grey government took office, Palmerston was its Secretary of State for Foreign Affairs.

2
INTERESTS BUT NO ENTANGLEMENTS

Almack's Club may have been abuzz with gossip about filling places in the new Whig Cabinet in November 1830, but across Europe the talk was of revolution again challenging the old order. Greece had its independence guaranteed by the Great Powers in February 1830, but questions about her new boundaries with the Turks still remained. In August 1830, the Belgians rose against the Dutch control imposed by the Vienna settlement of 1815. Before the year had ended, the contagion of the July revolution reached Poland, and by 1831 it moved rebellious Germans and Italians to action. Each of these convulsions invited a reactionary response from Russia, Austria and Prussia, and threatened to shake the delicate balance of powers which had been constructed in 1815. Meanwhile, struggles in Portugal and Spain remained unresolved.

Despite his years in the War Office, Palmerston's governmental experience had not fully prepared him for the array of events surfacing across Europe. Nevertheless, the new Foreign Secretary had little choice in addressing the Belgian crisis at the outset. A conference of the great powers had already been scheduled in London in early November 1830 before the Whigs took office. As host of this gathering Palmerston was catapulted into the limelight, providing him with both the opportunity and the challenge to shape the outcome of the conference. It was a challenge for this neophyte who had to face men of experience like the skilful Frenchman Charles Talleyrand. The opportunity arose as chair of the conference, since this position allowed Palmerston to control and direct the London deliberations.

The Belgian struggle for independence from Dutch control was rooted in a past coloured by religious, cultural and political differences. Although separation was not inevitable, the lines of division between north and south arose as a result of the war that followed Philip II of Spain's attempt to enforce his authority in the 1560s. In contrast to the free Dutch, the Belgians had passed from the overseership of Spain to that of Austria, and then Revolutionary and Napoleonic France, until it was reunified with the United Netherlands at the Congress of Vienna. None of these territorial settlements reflected the wishes of the Belgian people. Not surprisingly, the Belgians, already separated from the Dutch by language and religion and further alienated by the heavy-handed rule of their king, William of Nassau, were bent on secession.

Although the Duke of Wellington's instinct would have been to defend the creation of the Dutch union of 1815, he realized that Belgium independence was inevitable.[1] Fearful that King Louis-Philippe's new government in France would exploit the situation by coming to Belgium's aid against the Dutch, the Duke wisely recommended negotiations among all the parties. He therefore urged the London Conference, already meeting to discuss the problems in Greece, to turn its attention to the crisis in the Low Countries.

When Palmerston entered the scene, the way had already been paved for him to shape a particular solution to the Belgian crisis. For Palmerston, Belgian independence and neutrality were 'irreversible'.[2] The crucial issue before the conference was how the Belgian settlement could be realized so as to preserve the balance of power and prevent a war between the Eastern Powers and a resurgent France. Palmerston may have been sympathetic to the Belgian people's quest for self-determination as he was in support of liberal causes generally. But such questions were peripheral to more pressing British interests,[3] namely the prevention of French hegemony in the area, including access to Antwerp and the Scheldt estuary. Palmerston also knew that French intervention on behalf of the Belgians would move King William to seek help from Prussia, with Austria and Russia later joining the fray. Hoping to avoid a war, most European statesmen, despite their own inclinations, favoured a neutral, independent Belgium as the best guarantee of stability in the area.[4]

By the Protocol of 20 December 1830, the Great Powers recognized Belgium as an independent constitutional monarchy and not a republic. This overturning of the Dutch union of 1815 was a concession that even the Austrians and Russians could make, but allowing a republic to be formed was unthinkable, considering the impact it would have on Italy and Poland where revolutionary rumbles could be felt. Even Palmerston and Louis-Philippe favoured a monarchy, the latter wishing to keep his own nation rallied around the monarchial principle.

There was no lack of candidates for the Belgian throne, with three names mentioned most prominently. At the outset, the Belgians recoiled at any thought of having the Dutch King William's son, the Prince of Orange, as their sovereign. They had considered the Duke of Leuchtenberg, who had Bonapartist connections, and Louis-Philippe's son, the Duke of Nemours. Leuchtenberg's Bonapartist ties made him unacceptable to the Orleanists in France and to the great powers as well. The Belgians, with enthusiastic support from the French, favoured Nemours and elected him on 3 February 1831.[5] On 8 February, Palmerston seized the initiative by putting the French on notice that the Belgian offer to Nemours had to be refused or they would risk war with Britain. Rather than embarrass Louis-Philippe with a direct ultimatum, Palmerston cleverly put this threat in a memorandum to Lord Granville, the English ambassador in Paris, knowing that French intelligence would see it. Although such warnings evoke images of gunboat diplomacy, Palmerston placed the burden on the French by allowing them to choose between peace and war.[6] On the following day, the French king intervened to turn down the invitation to his son.[7] To be sure, Palmerston would have been able to rally the support of the great powers if France had not given way, but in early 1831 the attention of Britain's allies was diverted by revolutionary uprisings in Germany, Italy and Poland. Moreover, in retreating, Louis-Philippe had to abandon the quest for much-needed prestige. In taking this bold first step, it would be difficult to underestimate the dangers Palmerston courted in an effort to protect Belgian independence.

A second diplomatic victory came for Palmerston in his nomination of Leopold of Saxe-Coburg for the Belgian throne, but it was a victory coupled with a challenge. Unburdened by any direct ties to the Great Powers, Leopold was seen by Palmerston as the ideal neutral candidate to lead a neutral nation.[8] However, Leopold's nomination did not ensure his easy acquiescence to the final settlement in Belgium. On 20 January 1831, the London Conference agreed to the *Bases de Séparation*. Under this agreement, the boundaries between Holland and Belgium were restored to those of 1790, with the Dutch receiving the Grand Duchy of Luxemburg. Leopold, seeking a buffer zone against invasion, refused to sacrifice Luxemburg as part of the settlement. Initially,

Palmerston stood firmly against this demand but after several months of wrangling, the British gave way, rescinding the *Bases de Separation* and replacing it with eighteen articles which recognized Belgian control of Luxemburg. Palmerston had feared that Leopold would never take the throne unless his demands were met. Without Leopold on the throne, Palmerston reasoned, the Belgians would be tempted to form a republic which, in turn, would renew the struggle against the Netherlands and become a citadel for revolutionary activity in Europe.[9] He later explained to the Dutch king that unless this concession was made, a renewal of hostilities would follow, with the French entering the fray as an ally of Belgium.[10]

This reversal by Palmerston only moved King William to end the armistice with Belgium by sending his troops cross the Belgian border on 1 August 1831. This incursion triggered retaliation by the French who forced the Dutch troops to withdraw. Faced with a barrage of Tory criticism at home for allowing the French to exploit the situation,[11] Palmerston shifted his focus from the Dutch danger to a French one. It was one thing to deal with King William's stubborn efforts to undo the Belgian settlement, but now the 1815 safeguards against a revived France were threatened. Nor did it take long for Palmerston to realize that French meddling in the Low Countries represented a direct threat to British interests as well. Using the same strategy employed to keep a French candidate off the Belgian throne in February, Palmerston let it be known by 17 August that the only alternative to French withdrawal was war.[12] Again the French retreated, withdrawing their troops before the end of August. With France put in its place, Palmerston, working tirelessly day and night, was able to win a settlement from the London Conference to replace both the rejected *Bases de Separation* of January 1831 and the eighteen articles originally agreed to on 26 June 1831. With Belgium's independence and neutrality already assured, minor restrictions were placed on her control of Luxemburg to please the Dutch. In turn, they had to evacuate Antwerp, so strategically important to the British, and the Scheldt River was freed for navigation by all nations.[13] For all intents and purposes, the crisis in Belgium was over. Some nations delayed before ratifying the treaty, with the Dutch stubbornly holding out until 1839. But few doubted that it was a victory for Belgium and for Palmerstonian diplomacy as well.

The challenge of dealing with his diplomatic counterparts in 1831 had been daunting. Palmerston was a mere novice compared with men like Talleyrand of France, Austria's Prince Esterhazy and Ambassador

Lieven of Russia. Still, despite manoeuvring both inside and outside the conference rooms, Palmerston's control over details and events was unchallenged. Drawing upon his experience at the War Office, he set an exhausting pace for his lieutenants in preparing the conference agenda and keeping the delegates on task. From the time they met in November 1830 until their final deliberations one year later, he drove them to exhaustion by focusing on the finer points of boundary disputes, custom regulations and complicated financial arrangements. More importantly, from the outset it was Palmerston who tenaciously controlled the direction and purpose of the conference, keeping it centred on solving the crisis in the Low Countries. Using a combination of coaxing and cajolery, he shepherded the conference delegates to do his will. Certainly, his ability to keep the French from making mischief in Belgium was crucial to Britain's vital interests as well as the Great Powers' concerns about maintaining the 1815 settlement. Again, in September 1831, it was with the same self-confidence that he boldly demanded that the French leave Belgium after adroitly taking advantage of their presence there to frighten the Dutch into evacuating the area. Was this a precursor of Palmerstonian sabre rattling? Or was he diplomatically warning the French that the Belgian crisis was not without hazards, including the prospect of war?

It was a further measure of Palmerston's achievement that he was able to use the French threat as a way of prying concessions from the Eastern Powers. Not surprisingly, the Austrians, Russians and Prussians shrank from undermining the 1815 accords by tolerating Belgian independence won through revolution. It was bad enough that a man of Metternich's stature had allowed the initiative to slip into Palmerston's inexperienced hands at the London Conference. In point of fact, Palmerston gained from the chagrined Eastern Powers more than even he had bargained for. When the conference delegates agreed to Belgium's independence, Palmerston got more than a guarantee of friendship; he received recognition of Belgian neutrality. This concession, which Palmerston called 'an immense thing done', precluded the need for any explicit guarantee protecting Belgium from aggression.[14] Instead, the treaty had the self-abnegating effect of preventing any of the powers from taking advantage of Belgium, a safeguard aimed obviously at French designs.[15]

In the process of facing the challenges posed by the Belgium crisis, Palmerston began charting a course for himself in foreign affairs. It was enough of an accomplishment that in this first diplomatic venture he was a masterful host of the London Conference, acting painstakingly to broker relations between the parties. However, his greater achievement lay in using persuasion mingled with boldness to advance British interests without becoming ensnared in entanglements. The realization of an independent and neutral Belgium exemplified this success.

In championing Belgium's cause for independence Palmerston was motivated less by his altruistic liberal principles and more by the desire to maintain Europe's fragile balance of power. His support for Greek independence from the Turks was consistent with this view. Palmerston did not want to undermine the sovereignty of the Ottoman Turks and thereby leave the eastern Mediterranean vulnerable to Russian influence, so he favoured the creation of a Greece free from Tsarist designs. To ensure against Russian hegemony he demanded that Greece have defensible borders that would follow a line from the Gulf of Arta to the Gulf of Volo, including Arcanania and Aetolia. Once these changes were agreed to by the summer of 1832, Palmerston then argued in a speech to the House of Commons that Greek independence was necessary in serving the interest of Britain as well as that of civilization.[16]

In dealing with Greece and Belgium, Palmerston's bold strokes at the London Conference were strikingly different in execution but cautiously consistent with his predecessors' foreign policy prescriptions. Over time, both Castlereagh and Canning had quit the Congress System rather than allow any power to intervene or commit aggression in another country on the pretext of stifling internal revolution. Palmerston also opposed outside interference with another country's attempts at internal reforms: witness his non-interventionist response to France's July 1830 Revolution. But then he stood Castlereagh and Canning's non-interventionism on its head by reasoning that intervention sparked by revolutionary enthusiasm from a neighbouring country had to be combated if it endangered a nation's sovereignty and, ultimately, the peace of Europe.[17]

Palmerston's achievement in the Low Countries in 1831 seemed to lie in his ability to make the Eastern Powers realize that British interests in containing France were also in Europe's best interests. Ironically, in recognizing Belgium's revolutionary effort and resultant independence, he was able to persuade the delegates at the London Conference that they were indeed adhering to the 1815 settlement by safeguarding the balance of power and the peace of Europe. His goals were, therefore, essentially conservative without being obscurantist and reactionary.

Although preoccupied with the Belgian situation, Palmerston had to respond to other crises looming elsewhere in Europe. Just as the prevention of war had been his central concern in the Low Countries, he viewed the revolutionary upheavals occurring in Italy, Poland and Germany in 1830–1 as dress rehearsals for more explosive confrontations. When liberals rose up in Romagna against the reactionary Pope Benedict XVI in February 1831, Palmerston once again feared that the French could exploit the revolutionary cause in an effort to reclaim their lost Napoleonic hegemony in Italy. At the same time, he did not want to support Metternich in suppressing constitutional movements.[18] Also, it would not have been politic to appear to be protecting the Pope when anti-papal sentiments were running high in England. Communicating through his unofficial intermediary, Sir Brook Taylor, Palmerston tried to impress upon the Holy See the value of granting reforms that would deflate revolutionary pressures. Unfortunately, the Pope was deaf to his appeals.[19]

By the end of 1832, the Hapsburgs remained secure in their positions in Italy, and the Austrians and the French, despite their shows of strength, had not come to blows. This may be partially attributable to Palmerston's persuasive powers since he cautioned both sides that a confrontation in Italy could lead to a wider war – something neither Louis-Philippe nor Metternich wanted.[20] The Italian crisis seemed more perilous in Piedmont where the prospects for a confrontation between Austria and France were more evident than in the Papal States. Learning from the Belgian experience, the government in Turin thought that they could count on Britain to protect them if endangered by a French invasion. Palmerston, in trying to remain faithful to non-interventionism, made it clear that any commitment by the British government would be aimed at keeping both the French and the Austrians out of Piedmont. Unable to count on Palmerston for a military guarantee against the French, Turin looked to Vienna for a defensive pact. Meanwhile, France, distracted by news of the Dutch invasion of Belgium in August 1831, delayed any hostilities in Piedmont.[21]

As in Belgium, revolutionary discontents in Italy tested Palmerston's newly found talents at maintaining the balance of power and the peace of Europe. In Belgium's case, as host of the London Conference, Palmerston could address a crisis that was a real potential danger to Britain's vital interests. However, it strained the imagination of his fellow Whigs to suggest that the same pressing interests lay in Italy. Since threats, benign advice and concessions had no effect on the Pope and Austria, France realized that their actions could be undertaken with impunity. However, of the two powers in Italy it was Austria rather than France that represented a threat to the peace of Europe. From Palmerston's perspective, self-reform, especially of the Papal States, was the way to respond to revolutionary declarations. Without reform efforts to appease agitators, popular disturbances would follow. Austria would then have the pretext to intervene.

Palmerston also speculated that the Eastern Powers hoped that imminent hostilities in Italy would have the effect of aborting the Belgian settlement.[22] Palmerston's desire to balance his sympathy towards constitutional change with a cautious respect for order was also tested when the Poles had risen up against the Russians in November 1830. Unlike the situation in Italy, where Palmerston had at least made an effort to persuade the Pope to carry out reforms, he was for the most part unresponsive to the Poles. Certainly, he had a legal pretext to challenge the Tsar, for the 1815 Vienna accords required some consultation with the signatories before punitive action could be taken. The French, too, responding to what now had blossomed into a popular cause, urged Palmerston to act jointly in mediating the Russian–Polish conflict.[23]

Too many factors, however, dictated against any sort of intervention. Fearful that Jacobinical forces might exploit the Warsaw insurrection, Palmerston cautioned against British involvement.[24] Championing the Polish cause would have further jeopardized the tenuous relationship between Britain and Russia at a time when the Tsar's support was still needed as a deterrent against French meddling in Belgium. Palmerston could not afford to alienate St Petersburg as well as Vienna and Berlin when their cooperation at the London Conference was essential. Considered from another angle, having the Tsar's forces bogged down in Poland as the Austrian army was diverted in Italy meant that the Dutch had to confront Palmerston with a weaker hand.

Palmerston tried to distance himself from Polish matters throughout most of 1831, but by 1832 he could no longer avoid the groundswell of outrage against Russia's conduct that dominated parliamentary business both before and after the Easter recess. Radicals such as Joseph Hume and his ally Daniel O'Connell vented their anger at Palmerston, calling for the protection of Poland's constitution against the Russian barbarians.[25] Only the sober realization that the possible result of their criticism might be to return the Tories to power quieted them. Appeals by Polish *émigrés* were also to no effect. Throughout, Palmerston resolutely held the view that to help the Poles would require a British war with Russia, which was not in their mutual interest.[26] He could not have said it more clearly when he told the Polish aristocrat Prince

Czartoryski that, 'Now the English nation is able to make war, but it will only do so where its own interests are concerned.'[27] From Palmerston's standpoint, his treatment of the Russians proved profitable for Britain. Not only was a costly confrontation with Russia avoided, but also the Tsar's leverage could still be used against the Dutch king's stubborn refusal to sign the Belgian accords. In addition, any French plans to upset the status quo could be checked by an appeal to St Petersburg.

Palmerston's reluctance to criticize repression in Poland was matched by his slowness to speak out against the German Diet's passage of six resolutions restricting freedoms in the Germanic Confederation. The resolutions had been passed in response to agitation at the Hambach Festival in May 1832, when students drank a toast to Count Lafayette and made revolutionary speeches. Palmerston saw Metternich's hand in all of this as an intriguer intervening in the guise of a champion of order and reaction.[28] If Metternich overreacted in Germany, Palmerston reasoned, then France, feeling threatened by Austria, would be slow to retreat in Belgium.

However, his fear of Metternich upsetting the balance of power in Europe did not mean that Britain should play a more active role in Germany, any more than intervention was necessary on behalf of the Poles. Palmerston's hesitancy to act was no doubt influenced by William IV's decision as King of Hanover to join the other Diet members in voting for the six resolutions. But this was not Palmerston's final word on the subject. On 2 August 1832, in answer to a parliamentary resolution condemning the action of the German Diet, Palmerston admitted that the British people could not be indifferent to the status of independent constitutional states. With ringing clarity he made one of his most Palmerstonian statements: he considered 'the constitutional states to be the natural allies of this country; and whoever may be in office conducting the affairs of Great Britain, I am persuaded that no English ministry will perform its duty if it be inattentive to the interests to such states.'[29] Undoubtedly, these words were intended for more than the House of Commons members. Austrian agents conveyed the message to Vienna and, despite Metternich' s censorial efforts, some 200,000 copies were circulated in Germany.[30] This was hardly a case of sabre rattling, but Palmerston made it clear that the English government felt duty bound to speak out on such matters while denying any plans for armed intervention.[31] Softening his language in a later dispatch to the German Diet, he said that he was merely suggesting that it was in the best interests of their governments not to alienate their own people through these restrictive decrees. Instead, he advised that they calm discontent with the promise of constitutional guarantees.[32]

Predictably, the dispatch intensified the anger of the Eastern Powers. Metternich dismissed it out of hand and suppressed its publication. The Prussians refused to even receive it.[33] The Prussians' rejection of Palmerston's statement was a sign that Berlin had succumbed to Metternich's reactionary policies. Being tied to Austria meant that Prussia was not free at this point to assist in the Belgian settlement or any other effort to maintain the balance of power peacefully. Palmerston also believed that Prussia should be open to change and thus be able to adapt peacefully to the needs of its people. Speaking of all nations, and especially of Germany's future, he said in 1833, at a time when Prussian and Austrian troops were suppressing uprisings in Frankfurt, 'The province of a wise Govt [sic] is to keep pace with the improved notions of the people....Thus to render safe and tranquil those changes which if made violently might be dangerous – to lead & direct, and not to hold back till a superior force drags them along.'[34]

To all appearances, Palmerston's efforts at redirecting events in Germany were a failure, but to some historians his words first uttered in early August 1832 were filled with implications for the future. Donald Southgate calls his statements a 'Dramatic departure from the norms of diplomacy' and 'a species of diplomatic revolution', while Jasper Ridley claims that 'Palmerston took the first step on the road to become the accepted champion of Liberalism in Europe.'[35] It may have been difficult to convince the parliamentary radicals in 1832-3 that Palmerston was fighting for democratic causes around the world, but, in a larger context, his words and actions were defining moments in British foreign policy. Eschewing overt interference in the internal affairs of countries such as Poland and Germany, Palmerston felt obliged to at least use words as a substitute for arms. He set forth in no uncertain terms Britain's friendly disposition towards duly constituted regimes. Like his predecessors, Castlereagh and Canning, he upheld the territorial guarantees laid down at Vienna in 1815. There, to ensure such guarantees, they had chosen the safer course of non-interference as a maxim for all signatories. Palmerston, desiring to maintain the territorial status quo, appears to have raised the stakes. He feared that Metternich's search for order would promise only the peace of the graveyard and drive agitators to violent extremes. Palmerston realized that as a great power Great Britain could not be a passive on-looker. Once he identified Britain's own interests with the maintenance of peace in Europe as a whole, he then took the next step of recognizing that a threat to the status quo came more from the champions of order than from exponents of change. In articulating this position, Palmerston had cleverly turned the tables on Metternich. The message from Vienna had consistently been that revolutionary movements, even the prospect of constitutional change, were threats to Europe's stability. Palmerston, like Metternich, had made peace and order his first concern and he, too, saw revolutionaries as a threat. But he did not confuse these dangers with groundswells for necessary reform. Indeed, the sentiments expressed in his speech of 2 August 1832 were that constitutional states were Britain's natural allies precisely because they were preventing revolution by addressing the people's grievances. He argued that Metternich's formula to use the weapons of order was a prescription for disorder leading to disastrous consequences.[36]

While diplomats wrestled with unrest across the continent, at home debates in Parliament centred on the Whigs' reform bill. Introduced in the House of Commons by Lord John Russell in March 1831, it called for major alterations in the representative and electoral system. Although radical expectations of a wider franchise were not met, Russell shocked many members when he announced the abolition of 168 boroughs, replacing them with only 43 new boroughs. In addition to 40-shilling freeholders, the vote was also extended to household occupiers whose houses were worth £10 a year. Although still favouring property-owners, the fact that some 500,000 voters had been added to a dramatically changed representative system delighted even the radicals and further alienated the ultra-Tories.

Palmerston's views on the Reform Bill fell somewhere between these positions. As a Canningite, he had been open to change. When he chose to join the Grey ministry in November 1830, there was no question that he had jumped on the reform coach.[37] While he could not easily be put in the same camp as such liberal Whigs as Lord Althorp, Russell and Lord Durham, he was comfortable in following the centrist views of Grey and Melbourne. When he spoke in support of the bill on 3 March 1831, he said that while the ancient constitution had served the English people well, he recognized that reform must be adopted to avoid revolution. He even saw value in adding the talents of the middle class to the House's membership so long as it was understood that the traditional role of the aristocracy would remain inviolate.[38] Although Palmerston had hoped that more restrictions would be placed on the bill, he felt that if it failed the countryside would be ablaze with violence.[39] He thought the only recourse was moderation won by carefully negotiated compromise.

However, when the bill was passed by only one vote in March and then suffered successive setbacks in April, Grey decided to appeal to the people in a general election. While the May elections returned a greater Whig majority, Palmerston did not fare as well in Cambridge. William Cavendish, a traditional Whig, siphoned off votes from Palmerston, leaving him last in a four-man race. The Tory candidates, Sir Robert Peel and Henry Goulburn, prevailed with 805 and 804 votes respectively; Cavendish received 630, while Palmerston trailed with 610. Ironically, he found a safe seat in Bletchingley, which would be abolished once the Whig bill was passed.[40]

While Palmerston was losing in Cambridge, the Whigs and the reform movement were riding a crest of victory. Not surprisingly, when Parliament returned after the election, the Reform Bill passed through the Commons easily – only to be thrown out by the Lords. The country was outraged, and again there was talk of revolution. At this point, the only alternative was to ask the King to create new peers, since further concessions were out of the question. This time Palmerston led the way by recommending such action to the King if the Lords again rejected the bill. However, it was the King himself who stood in the way by refusing to go along with the scheme. The Whigs then resigned which brought in Wellington to fashion a Tory ministry. The uproar in the country that followed made the Tory effort shortlived. The radical Francis Place's call for a run on the banks accompanied by wholesale violence and the imminent threat of revolution sufficed to force the King to recall Grey and accept the Whig's demands. The Lords were forced to pass the bill on 4 June, which received the royal assent on 7 June 1832.[41]

Palmerston's position on the parliamentary reform bill sheds light on what Donald Southgate calls his practice of concessionary conservatism. As a practical matter, Palmerston believed that one must reform in a timely way in order to preserve. Following a rule fostered by George Canning, he knew that it was better to make moderate concessions in peacetime rather than be forced to accede to greater demands in the midst of revolutionary tumult. But there were limits to what Palmerston would accept. For the Radicals, 1832 only signalled the beginning of additional reform efforts. However, for Palmerston, like Lord John Russell, the 1832 Act was the final concession to the unenfranchised.[42] As an aristocrat, he had always championed the Whig principle that the popular will must be filtered though a social hierarchy of experienced statesmen and politicians. It is important to remember, however, that Palmerston was also a man driven more by events than by doctrinal beliefs. It is true that no major electoral reforms were forthcoming until after Palmerston's death in 1865, but anti-reformist instincts did not prevent him from bowing to necessity in order to prevent revolution.[43]

In Eastern courts the Reform Bill's passage was considered to have the stamp of the British Foreign Secretary on it. The same man, they thought, who had shepherded the Belgian settlement, and had called for constitutional concessions in Italy and Germany in 1831 and 1832, was conspiring with his fellow Whigs to revolutionize the British government. Meanwhile, at home, Palmerston continued to be the favourite target of the Tories. They reminded him that he had betrayed his former party and was now recklessly abandoning the foreign policy crafted at Vienna in 1815.

If the Tories were not attacking Palmerston, then the Radicals were pillorying him. Despite his image in foreign capitals, it would have been hard to convince men like Joseph Hume or Colonel de Lacy Evans that Palmerston was a champion of liberal changes in Europe and a true reformer at home. The Radicals focused instead on his seeming tolerance of repression in Poland or the curtailment of freedom in Germany. Nor did Palmerston win any accolades when the Reform Bill was passed since his support seemed at best begrudging. If these differences with the Radicals were not enough, his position as a spokesman for the government in the House of Commons made him the target of constant attacks. Unlike his days in Opposition when he could speak openly, now as Foreign Secretary his speeches tended to be cautious or cloaked in guarded language. Nor did it help that his still unschooled statements were punctuated with stammers, stutters and rhetorical flourishes that seemed to lead nowhere, a situation made worse by his tendency to assume a pompous air, and made even more obnoxious by his dandified appearance.[44]

With the dissolution of the House after the Reform Bill's passage, Palmerston had to search for a new seat. He was finally able to find a county seat in the familiar locale of South Hampshire where he had some influence. Despite a raucous campaign in which he was subjected to charges of undue influence at the polls, he nevertheless succeeded, winning with 1625 votes. Another Whig candidate also won with 1539 votes, over a sole Tory who lost with 1276 votes.[45]

Although Palmerston's arch-critics, both Tories and Radicals, were frustrated in their efforts to dislodge him from the Foreign Office, the greater danger for him was a divided Grey ministry. There already was developing a widening gap between liberal Whigs, who favoured a more extensive parliamentary reform bill, and more cautious Cabinet members, such as Grey, Melbourne and Palmerston. When the Irish question re-emerged in 1833, the Whigs tried to calm Irish Catholic agitation with the combined remedies of coercion and conciliation. An Irish Coercion Bill was moved in Parliament that was balanced by talk of relief for Irish Catholics from paying tithes to support the established church. When the Coercion Bill was passed without the tithe reform, liberal Whigs such as Durham and Russell rebelled. A compromise could not be reached and there was talk of the Cabinet breaking up. A crisis loomed by the spring of 1834, with Russell and his friends pitted against the cautious Stanley, Sir James Graham and Viscount Goderich, all friends of Palmerston. Palmerston warned against the perils of any change, believing that the Tories would be too weak to last and the Radicals were an unthinkable alternative. Furthermore, Palmerston could not envision a combined effort by those who had favoured parliamentary reform and those who had opposed it. Given these unwelcome alternatives, he recommended the reconstruction of the present ministry, but it was too fragile to go on. By July 1834 the King turned to Robert Peel to form a Tory government.[46]

In order to shore up his numbers in the Commons, Peel had to risk dissolution and he went to the country in January 1835. Palmerston had been relatively confident that he would succeed again in South Hampshire as he had done in 1832. To his surprise, the election poll of mid-January 1835 turned out badly for him, leaving him in third place behind two Tory candidates. His poor showing may have been attributable to several reasons: he was no longer a government candidate and he had to share the Whig vote with Sir George Staunton who, like Palmerston, had won in 1832. Palmerston attributed his loss to his supporters' tardiness in getting out the vote and the zealotry of his Tory opponents. There was also some speculation that the Tories had been effective in frightening the local clergy with the spectre of their tithes being endangered by the Whigs.[47] When the 1835 Tory election returns proved insufficient to sustain Peel's government, Melbourne was asked to return, with the expectation that Palmerston would go to the Foreign Office. But to be in the government, he needed a seat in Parliament. He was eventually offered a seat at Tiverton so long as he paid the Whig incumbent not to run. In June he ran uncontested and would thereafter sit for Tiverton for the rest of his life.

Returning to the House of Commons was not as great a challenge as the prospect of trying to reclaim the Foreign Office in a Cabinet reconstituted by Lord Melbourne. Palmerston's enemies, including Whigs who had revelled in the news of his defeat in South Hampshire, thought that his days were over as Foreign Secretary. Lord Durham, with his own eyes on the Foreign Office, together with his ally Edward Ellice persisted in their criticism of Palmerston. However, Durham's radical views frightened Melbourne too much to make him a likely replacement for Palmerston.[48]

Even Melbourne was troubled by Palmerston's interventionist tendencies. Pettier criticisms from smaller minds focused on Palmerston's lack of punctuality, indifference to the forms of diplomatic etiquette, and impatience with the idle chatter of the salon. When other positions were offered to Palmerston, he refused, arguing that for him to leave the Foreign Office would signal a change in foreign policy. Of course, if no place was found for him, then he might reappear in opposition as a critic of an alternative foreign policy. Despite all these concerns, Melbourne turned again to Palmerston, who resumed his duties as Foreign Secretary on 26 April 1835.[49]

Upon his return, no problem seemed more intractable than the civil strife in the Iberian Peninsula. In his seminal speech on interventionism of 1 June 1829, Palmerston had laid out his approach to Iberian affairs when railing against Wellington's tolerance of Dom Miguel's deposition of his niece, the Portuguese Queen Maria in 1828.[50] This was the prescriptive language that would guide Palmerston in his advocacy of constitutional regimes embattled against absolutism even if it required British interference in a country's internal affairs. The Tories had been following Canning's policy of non-intervention although Wellington had at least cut diplomatic ties with Miguel's government.[51] This did not satisfy Palmerston, who told the House of Commons that Britain had been involved in 'one unbroken chain' of meddling with Portugal's government since 1807.[52]

If Palmerstonian interventionism was acceptable in Portugal, then why was it not used in Spain? In Madrid, a succession crisis developed in September 1833 with the death of King Ferdinand VII. His successor was his daughter Isabella, aged three. Because of her minority, her mother Maria Cristina of Naples served as regent and in that capacity established a constitutional government. Isabella's uncle, Don Carlos, a claimant to the throne before the birth of his niece, opposed her succession and the liberalizing tendencies of her mother. The Spanish Catholic Church and the Eastern Powers, which were already committed to defending conservative regimes in Europe, supported Don Carlos' claim.

The boldness of Palmerston's speech in 1829 did not match his actions in office in 1830, particularly with regard to Iberian affairs. While he did not hesitate to sponsor the independence of Belgium from Holland, he treated parallel events occurring in Portugal and Spain more cautiously. From the outset in Portugal, he declared a policy of strict neutrality towards the growing struggle between Dom Miguel and those of his brother, Dom Pedro. Palmerston had re-affirmed his neutral stance, but he encouraged Miguel to grant amnesty to his opponents.[53] Moreover, official detachment from the struggle did not keep Palmerston from forcefully defending the interests of Britain which had been formalized by long-standing treaty provisions guaranteeing the rights of British subjects in Portugal. This became the thin edge of the wedge, permitting greater British intervention in the growing opposition to Miguel. By 1832, he tacitly allowed British volunteers to assist Dom Pedro's forces, particularly Admiral Sir Charles Napier who defeated Miguel's fleet in early 1833. A brutal war followed until Miguel capitulated. Queen Maria was restored to the throne and she promised to follow the liberal constitution of 1822.

Palmerston's achievement in Portugal was modest compared to what he called 'a capital hit' in Spain.[54] When Don Carlos attempted to intervene in Portugal on Miguel's side in 1833, Palmerston joined the French in the following April to sign the Quadruple Alliance. Palmerston had declined to assist the French in 1831 in defeating Dom Miguel, but now the danger of a joint effort by Carlos and Miguel seemed more ominous. Moreover, it was possible that France might intervene in Spain without British assistance. By this agreement, signed on 22 April 1834, Isabella's troops (assisted by the British navy) effectively defeated absolutism in Spain and Portugal and thereby opened the way for more liberal governments to flourish. With the help of Palmerston, Carlos withdrew in defeat to England, only to return furtively to Spain to renew the civil war with greater savagery against Isabella's forces.

Looming over military victory in Portugal and Spain were the diplomatic implications of the Quadruple Alliance. Practising what has been called 'cooperative restraint', Palmerston had masterfully controlled

French instincts to exploit the situation in the Iberian Peninsula. Earlier, this tactic had worked in Belgium when he used the French to chase the Dutch back into Holland. More importantly, it has been argued, by aligning France, Spain, Portugal and Britain, Palmerston had established a diplomatic counterpoise to the Eastern Powers. In short, a balance of power now existed between Austria, Russia and Prussia (those nations most inclined to support absolutist regimes) and the Western Powers (who could be counted on to foster the growth of constitutionalism). From Palmerston's standpoint, this entente with France was a welcome alternative to Castlereagh's older Quadruple Alliance, which entangled Britain, Austria, Prussia and Russia as strange bedfellows.

Support for the Quadruple Alliance in general did not always translate into an unqualified defence of Queen Isabella in practice. As noted, Carlos's return to Spain from England undid Palmerston's effort at peace-making. He was faithful to the Quadruple Alliance of 1833, but he remained only ambivalently committed to supporting Queen Isabella's liberal regime. Fearful that the use of a naval blockade in international waters against the Carlists risked incidents with some of the Eastern Powers, he refused any official involvement on the side of the queen's forces, the Isabelinos. Following Britain's example, Louis-Philippe also refused to endanger the lives of French troops in Spain. Palmerston was willing to follow the practice used earlier in Portugal, namely the relaxation of the Foreign Enlistment Acts by permitting mercenaries to join in defence of the Spanish government. Palmerston's support for the liberal regime, however, put him at odds with the parliamentary Opposition. In an effort to quiet the Tories, who defended the Carlist side, Palmerston made sure that this war would cost the British nothing. The financial burden, he insisted, would fall entirely on the Spanish government. The result was that as much time was spent collecting debts from Spain as energies were devoted to defeating the Carlist side. Similarly, Palmerston had to contend with divisions in the Isabelinos ranks between a radical faction and the moderate liberals. When France threw its support behind the moderates favoured by Christina, the Queen Regent, Palmerston backed the radicals who eventually seized power under the heavy-handed rule of General Baldomero Espartero.

The defeat of the Carlist forces in 1839, signalling the end of the civil war, was one more victory for constitutionalism over absolutism and, coupled with the restoration of a liberal regime in Portugal, it was also a triumph for Palmerstonian diplomacy. Certainly, British intervention had been crucial to the outcome in both states, but to suggest that Palmerston enjoyed an unqualified victory would be an exaggeration. The installation of a radical government in Madrid was not of Palmerston's making and he was disturbed by its democratizing tendencies. In addition, he failed to collect long-overdue debts from this government plagued by insolvency. Also, relations with Britain soured over the Portuguese slowness to give up the slave trade, a cause that Palmerston was attempting to enforce zealously. His free trade policies were also thwarted by a Portuguese attempt to impose duties on British imports.

On the face of it, Palmerston's Iberian policy was at least a limited success. He could boast that the victories of Queen Maria in Portugal and Isabella in Spain were triumphs for the establishment of free institutions and independence. By 'independence' he meant that they were free from outside influence, especially from France, and free to look to Britain for military and commercial assistance. He could also point to the Quadruple Alliance as both a successful deterrent against the Eastern Powers in the Iberian Peninsula and a mechanism to ensure the cooperation of France in safeguarding constitutionalism. Indeed, by embracing the French, he was able to exert control over them. Beneath this veneer of collaboration, however, were deeply ingrained mutual suspicions about each side's intentions towards the newly restored liberal regimes. Once moderate and radical factions began courting support from London and Paris, the old rivalries re-emerged, signalling a deterioration in Anglo-French relations. Palmerston would not retreat from upholding British interests in Spain or Portugal, but he knew that he ran the risk of jeopardizing the Alliance and also of driving France into the arms of the Eastern Powers. With this in mind, he told Lord Granville fatalistically to tell the French Premier, 'That we look upon France as backing out of the alliance as fast as she can, that we are sorry for it, but wash our hands of the consequences.'[55]

If Palmerston's interventionism in Spain and Portugal had tested the delicacy of Anglo-French relations, the Eastern Question would bring them to breaking point. The Eastern Question which raised questions about the fate of the Ottoman Empire was an issue that touched a nerve in most European capitals in the nineteenth century. The Turkish Sultan Mahmud II (1808–39) was trying to hold together an antiquated, corrupt supra-nation state in an environment seething with revolutionary nationalism. The Great Powers stood on the sidelines, waiting for the 'Sick Man of Europe' to collapse, so that they might opportunistically fill the resulting power vacuum.

Although Palmerston had already made his mark elsewhere, he would meet his greatest challenge in the Levant and achieve his greatest success to date as a master diplomat. His guiding principle remained the same: namely to pursue British interests above all else but to do so without becoming entangled in any long-standing international commitments. Even before he entered the Foreign Office, Palmerston had addressed matters in the Levant. In 1827, he spoke as a Canningite, favouring British support of Greek independence from the Turks. It was not the abstract idea of Greek liberty that interested him so much as the practical need to join Russia in assisting the Greeks lest the Tsar have his own way in the Balkans.[56] In 1829, his espousal of Greek independence set forth a clear blueprint for the future. Fearful that Russia might use its patronage of the Greeks to gain a free hand in the dying Ottoman Empire, Palmerston supported Canning's effort in 1827 to have Britain jointly sponsor Greek independence. This meant that when the Treaty of Adrianople recognized Greek independence, Greece became indebted not just to Russia but also to Britain and the Great Powers generally.

On becoming Foreign Secretary, Palmerston's interests in the Near East and the interplay of relations between Russia and the Ottoman Empire intensified. As British trade expanded in the eastern Mediterranean with the advent of the steamship, the fate of Turkey became critical for access to Suez, the Red Sea and ultimately to Asia. Although Palmerston was not unfriendly to Russia at this point in his career, he viewed its involvement in Asia, and especially Persia and Afghanistan, with suspicion. Moreover, he was sensitive to the shadow that Russia was casting over the Ottoman Empire and what this might mean to the balance of power in the region. The Russians, however, were not the only ambitious powers in the area who might accelerate the Turkish Empire's dismemberment and thereby bring on war. France was cultivating allies in the Middle East with the object of developing French naval hegemony in the Mediterranean.

One of those allies was Mehemet Ali, a *parvenu* Albanian, who rose from his lowly origins as a tobacco salesman to become a military adventurer for the Sultan. His ruthless military conquests stretched from Egypt, over which he became Pasha, south to the Sudan and Abyssinia. Although technically a vassal to the Sultan, Mehemet was poised to turn on his overlord by fracturing the Turkish empire and placing his son Ibrahim at its head. By 1832, Ibrahim had conquered Syria and was poised to attack Constantinople. Desperate for help, the Sultan sought assistance from other nations, including Britain. Palmerston's response to the Sultan's call was predictable for he saw that the empire was in imminent danger. Although Mehemet Ali's reputation as a modernizer might have appealed to Palmerston, he had a genuine dislike for this interloper. More importantly, Mehemet had stronger ties with France than he did with Britain. Consequently, a victory for Mehemet Ali against the Sultan would be seen as a victory for France and her ambitions in the eastern Mediterranean.

Palmerston cautioned against inaction as he felt that this would allow some other nation to seize the initiative in coming to the defence of the Sultan. Unfortunately, he was unable to persuade the Cabinet of the wisdom of his views. Although inclined to send the fleet to the Porte, Palmerston could not persuade the Cabinet to agree with him. The Reform Bill crisis had captured the Whigs' attention and the Francophiles among them were critical of taking any action against Mehemet Ali due to his modernizing reformist influence in North Africa. Moreover, the fleet, weakened by neglect since 1815, was already over-committed in the Low Countries and Portugal. Finally, one wonders whether Palmerston's own understanding of Britain's relationship with the Ottoman Empire had fully ripened into maturity. It has been argued that, with his attention on Western Europe, he did not fully grasp the implications of giving the Russians, the French and their surrogates free play in the East. Halevy suggested that Palmerston had tacitly allowed the French to take the lead in Constantinople by befriending the Sultan as a consolation prize for yielding during the Belgian crisis.[57] Whatever the underlying circumstances, Palmerston could not escape the fact that Britain had suffered a diplomatic setback at the hands of the Russians. His worst fears were confirmed when he heard news of the Treaty of Unkiar Skelessi of July 1833, under which the Turks permitted the Russians exclusive permission to sail their ships into the Sea of Marmora. This effectively meant that Russia had closed the Dardanelles to shipping and thereby commanded a Turkish protectorate. Indeed, it is possible that Unkiar Skelessi represented a turning-point in Palmerston's view of the Eastern Question and Anglo-Russian relations. Prior to 1833, he treated Russia with equanimity, believing that the Tsar had been cautious in his dealings with the Sultan. After Unkiar Skelessi, Palmerston was determined that Britain would not drop her guard again in the Levant. Hereafter in the nineteenth century his gaze remained fixed on Russia as the chief threat in the region against which Britain must vigilantly safeguard the Turkish Empire. Thus as a crisis loomed in the Crimea seventeen years later, there was a predisposition to blame Russia and a readiness to engage in hostilities against her.[58]

However, as events unfolded after 1833, there is little evidence that bellicosity influenced Anglo-Russian relations. The last thing that Palmerston wanted to do in the 1830s was to go to war with Russia, notwithstanding the drumbeat of criticism from radicals over the plight of the Poles. Despite his wariness of Russia, Palmerston believed a direct confrontation would produce a European war and a scramble for territory by those powers seeking to exploit the Sultan's vulnerability. Moreover, the Tsar, for his part, was eager to improve relations with Britain in the hope of detaching the British from both France and the Quadruple Alliance. Palmerston had resisted these blandishments, knowing that in order to limit the actions of the reactionary Eastern Powers he needed France as a counterweight. This worked best when liberal parties controlled France and pressure from French public opinion sustained the constitutionalism espoused by Palmerston. More conservative French politicians suspected Palmerston's liberal causes and saw that their own interests were at odds with those of Britain. Certainly, as both countries were drawn into the rival power plays that dominated Portuguese and Spanish politics in the 1830s, the ties that bound the Quadruple Alliance began to wear.

The option of turning from the French alliance to a Russian one was not realistic, but by 1839 events in the Near East opened the way for greater cooperation with St Petersburg. In that year, a dying Sultan Mahmud challenged Mehemet Ali's hold on Syria. Palmerston was slow to come to Mahmud's aid, fearing an escalation in hostilities. However, when he saw the French and Russians ready to align themselves with the opposing forces, he acted. He originally had agreed to join the French in sending their fleets to the Dardanelles but he first initiated a Great Power conference to try to pacify the region. The outcome of that meeting was the Collective Note of 27 July 1839. Under its provisions, Mehemet Ali was required to evacuate Syria and retire to Egypt. In return, and here was Palmerston's diplomatic masterstroke, Mehemet's family would be given hereditary rule in Egypt. It was a courageous concession on Palmerston's part for this action invited criticism from various quarters and it ran against his own instincts to punish Mehemet's wanton aggression. Negotiations over the implementation of the agreement dragged on into 1840, but in the end it was a victory for Palmerstonian diplomacy. From the outset, the Russians accepted the plan. Metternich hesitated, but eventually the Austrians went along. France, standing by their ally in North Africa, said no and suffered diplomatic isolation.

A key obstacle to Palmerston's plan also came from his own Cabinet where a minority of Francophile Whigs opposed his attempt to limit Mehemet Ali. There had been a consistent effort by Lord Holland (whose family's sympathies with the revolutionary tradition were well known) together with liberal Whigs to undermine Palmerston's foreign policy. The cautious Lord Melbourne had always had his doubts about Palmerston's bold ventures, but his first priority was stability within the government. When Palmerston tested his support in the Cabinet by offering his resignation on 5 July 1840, not surprisingly Melbourne rejected it.[59]

On 15 July 1840, representatives of four of the Great Powers and Turkey met in London to guarantee the security of the Turkish Empire. In addition, Mehemet Ali was required to withdraw from Syria and Crete but retained hereditary rule over Egypt, as well as control over Southern Syria and the fortress at Acre. The danger of a confrontation with France loomed on the horizon when Palmerston told the French that the July agreement was a *fait accompli*. However, the replacement of the hostile Adolphe Thiers as Premier with the friendlier François Guizot by the end of 1840 eased the way to some degree of rapprochement. In July 1841, after some face-saving discussion, France belatedly joined the other Great Powers in signing the Straits Convention. The compromise agreement with Mehemet Ali remained and, very importantly, it was settled that no foreign warship could enter the Dardanelles during peacetime, thus undoing whatever advantage Russia had enjoyed under the Treaty of Unkiar Skelessi.

There seemed to be little question that the Straits Convention again was a triumph for Palmerstonian interventionism. Palmerston had thwarted Mehemet Ali's ambitions in the Arab world and successfully ensured the survival of the dying Ottoman Empire for the next eighty years. He persuaded the Russians to relinquish their privileged power in the Near East by sharing it with the Great Powers. Palmerston made it easier for the Foreign Office to be less reliant on the French entente by galvanizing relations with Russia. By daring to use force, he demonstrated that he was willing to go beyond the conference table to uphold British interests – for, as he argued, these interests were also Europe's interests.

It would be a mistake to think that Palmerston's success in fashioning the Straits Convention in 1841 confirmed British power in the Middle East and, more specifically, protected her trade routes to India. Notwithstanding Anglo-Russian cooperation in curtailing Mehemet Ali's ambitions, Palmerston did not view complacently the Tsarist threat to the northern tier of states stretching from Constantinople through Persia to India. Laying at the gateway to India was the backwater state of Afghanistan, chronically troubled by tribal instability and vulnerable to external threats from Russia and Persia. As Russia grew closer to Persia in the 1830s, Palmerston realized that it was time to protect British interests by cultivating an Afghan alliance. This meant, however, choosing one warlord over another, with the forsaken party probably turning to Russia as an ally. What followed in 1838 was a disastrous war in which Britain suffered a humiliating defeat. By 1841, Britain, now led by the Tories, avenged its loss with the bloody reconquest of Kabul. But there was no doubt that the Palmerstonian interventionism which had so adroitly been employed against Mehemet Ali, had its limitations when used in the unfriendly Afghan environment. Nevertheless, so important was it to Britain that Afghanistan act as a buffer state protecting India from Russian designs that the British would return to fight another day.

While the Afghan war of 1838–42 represented a setback for Palmerstonian interventionism, it must be balanced against other challenges to Britain's expanding global empire. It was again to protect British interests that Palmerston fought a war with China in 1839 over trading rights – even if it meant implicating Britain in the unseemly sale of opium. At the heart of this looming conflict was Britain's abiding interest in maintaining an open door to trade with some 350,000,000 inhabitants. Chinese authorities were less open to the outside world and treated foreigners as inferior beings, harassing their merchants and consular officials. This mutually acrimonious situation between Britain and China was further aggravated by the fact that illegal trade in opium amounted to more that 50 per cent of British exports to China by 1833. Palmerston did not support the rampant smuggling of opium, but the John Bull in him refused to accept the arbitrary persecution of innocent British subjects. Attempts at reaching a negotiated settlement collapsed by November 1839 when a direct confrontation took place between Chinese junks and British warships. The British easily won the battle but not the peace. Instead, the war continued under the Tories' watch when they assumed office in 1841 and finally ended in 1842 with the Treaty of Nanking. Under the treaty, the Chinese ceded Hong Kong, paid war damages and compensated British merchants for the destruction of opium.[60]

While Palmerston's fortunes rose in these years, those of his Whig government fell. Lacking a majority in the House of Commons, the Whigs depended on support from Radicals and the Irish Catholics under Daniel O'Connell. That alliance was dependent on the Whigs continuing to advance reforms such as an enlargement of the franchise. When 'Finality' Jack Russell decided that the 1832 Parliamentary Reform Act was the final and not the first instalment of Whig reforms the alliance cracked. Weakened by the 1837 parliamentary elections, the Whigs stumbled on through the Bedchamber Crisis of 1839. A naïve but wilful Queen Victoria, upset at having to give up her Whig Ladies of the Bedchamber for Tory ones, blocked Peel's formation of a new government. A complacent Melbourne was persuaded to stay on, thus averting a constitutional crisis, but a vote of no confidence on the budget shortly afterwards ended his agony. Parliamentary elections followed, with the Tories winning with a comfortable margin of seats in the House of Commons.[61]

Unlike his fellow Whigs, Palmerston was re-elected successfully at Tiverton in 1841, testifying to his improved electioneering skills. Accompanied by his wife, the former Lady Cowper (his long-time mistress whom he married in 1839), he tried to divert the crowd's attention away from the unpopular New Poor Law. Although Palmerston could not easily escape the criticism of his Chartist opponent who accused him of being a supporter of the hated New Poor Law, his reputation as a zealous enforcer of the slave trade's abolition did help his standing. Palmerston was also keen to exploit the growing xenophobia that could be linked to his accomplishments abroad. Pointing to the recent French repression of tribesmen in Algeria, Palmerston contrasted the humane reputation of British troops abroad to the atrocities witnessed in North Africa. Ignoring the brutalities committed against the Irish by the British, or the Russians' harsh repression of the Poles, he painted himself as a humanitarian at the expense of the French, now so ill-favored in British foreign relations.

It has been noted that this carefully prepared campaign speech, directed at a well-cultivated press, signals the beginning of a new stage in his political life. Palmerston, the aristocrat transforming himself into a popular demagogue, was adapting himself to the times. Unable and unwilling to speak the language of his Chartist, working-class opponent, he played upon the baser instincts of popular chauvinism.[62] It afforded him a wide audience of people who, although alien to his aristocratic manners, were at home with the new humanitarian rhetoric charged with patriotic enthusiasm.

The Whigs may have left office in 1841, but Palmerston left behind his stamp on the Foreign Office. He had entered that office in 1830 as a relative neophyte, notwithstanding his years of experience as a subaltern in government. His 1829 speech had forecast his commitment to Canningite interventionism. In facing the unfinished business of Greek independence and the looming Belgian crisis, he began to redefine the meaning of diplomatic interventionism and how it would harness the revolutionary currents running throughout Europe. By 1841, his language and actions had dispelled any notion that disengagement from Europe was a diplomatic option open to Britain. Taking Canning's thinking to another level, he demonstrated that enforcement of the Vienna settlement and the maintenance of the balance of power required his active vigilance and outspoken assertion of British interests. Sometimes this took the form of promoting constitutional liberalism in Belgium or the Iberian Peninsula, and sometimes it involved the guarantee of treaty obligations in the Ottoman Empire. In almost every instance, he acted not in defence of abstract principles, but because inaction would jeopardize European stability, peace and freedom.

Palmerston had also used the 1830s to define the style as well as the substance of his diplomacy. If the newly coined term 'Palmerstonian' had a certain ring to it, it was because Palmerston made no distinction between his policies and the manner in which he pursued them. Although 'reckless' goes too far in describing Palmerston, diplomatic niceties seldom restrained him. The pace of Anglo-French negotiations over nominations for the Belgian throne, for example, quickened in 1831 once Palmerston suggested that hostilities might be the answer to Louis-Philippe's intransigence. In short, he seemed ready in these fledgling years to bring Britain to the brink of war. In going this far, he frightened the young Queen and alienated Francophile Whigs, who still questioned his commitment to Whiggery.

Palmerston's foreign policy goals were clear enough, but his Whig credentials did not satisfy all of his Cabinet colleagues. He may have possessed the title, land and the social connections to make him a candidate, but it took more than that to be a Whig. He had not shaken off his Tory ties but at the same time he didn't belong to the Foxite

Whig tradition. Consequently, his tough treatment of the new Orleanist regime made him suspect to the Francophile Whigs. It was precisely because his transition from being a Canningite had not reached its fulfilment in Whiggery that Palmerston's political evolution was still a work in progress. Palmerston's emerging primacy in foreign policy was readily discernible. The period from 1830 to 1841 marked the first phase of political alignments, culminating in the formation of the Liberal Party in 1858. Palmerston was still a political onlooker waiting to enter from the wings as a spokesman for the people. The 1830s may have provided him with the opportunity to thrust himself forward as an architect of foreign policy but, as Whigs and Tories struggled to articulate their own responses to the challenges of the Industrial Revolution, Palmerston's political future remained unclear.

3

THE REVOLUTIONARY CHALLENGE

As the Whigs fell from power, Palmerston's standing in the public eye began to rise. His espousal of Belgium independence and his willingness to speak out against arbitrary rule in Spain and Portugal won him liberal allies. Of course, his support for constitutional causes had to be reconciled with British interests and the maintenance of the balance of power. Palmerston's liberal credentials were based on his foreign policy initiatives, and he only favoured domestic reforms as long as they did not threaten his personal aristocratic order. His support for the cautions terms of the 1832 Reform Act, for example, guaranteed that the electoral system was still dominated by the social elite. Nevertheless, his guarded advocacy of political and economic reforms helped him to steal the Chartists' thunder at the hustings. However, as the 1840s proceeded, the question arose as whether such liberal gestures would be enough to satisfy the demands made by the 1848 revolutionaries. Liberal and nationalist stirrings in Italy, Prussia, Hungary and Poland, and their challenge to the 1815 settlement, tested the limits of Palmerston's outreach to liberalism. Given his disinclination to consider abstract questions, it is unlikely that he would rush to support liberal causes without considering their impact on Europe's stability.

Palmerston's growing reputation as a friend of liberalism stemmed in part from his enhanced image as a friend of the people. Increasingly, he used the public platform as an alternative to Westminster as the locus of political activity. Using chauvinistic rhetoric to make his appeal, he struck a chord with the crowd who seemed ready to have someone celebrate Britain's successes at home and abroad. Crucial for his appeal to the public was his clever use of the press. As early as 1834, he had cultivated ties with John Easthorpe, co-owner of the *Morning Chronicle*, who allowed him to use the newspaper as an organ of his views. It turned out to be a mutually beneficial arrangement, with favours, including invitations for weekends at Broadlands, monetary allowances, and other courtesies lavished on editors and reporters. No blandishment was too much to coax the press to his side, and the choice of correspondents covering his foreign assignments and his speeches on the hustings required his approval. In due course, the *Chronicle* and the *Globe* became his chief mouthpieces. Columns were literally dictated by Palmerston or had his imprint upon them. In time, most newspapers fell under Palmerston's influence. The *Morning Post* followed the example of the *Chronicle* and the *Globe* in remaining faithful to him throughout the mid-Victorian years. Even the *Times*, once it broke free from its Tory bias, joined Palmerston's column of supporters.[1]

Palmerston's standing may have risen in the public eye as the Whigs fell from power, but this did not mean that he was well liked by those who knew him best. Indeed, in the past eleven years, his reputation preceded him for offending others. His lack of diplomatic etiquette, his breezy and brusque treatment of ambassadors and even heads of state, and his duplicity were resented throughout the courts of Europe. In addition to his critics in the Cabinet, he was the target of relentless attacks from all political sides in Parliament. The ultra Tories still begrudged his abandonment of them in 1830 for the Whigs and his flirtation with liberal causes abroad. Among liberals the approach to Palmerston was divided. Those who followed Richard Cobden and John Bright under the banner of the Anti-Corn Law League agreed with Palmerston's free trade policies but detested his gunboat diplomacy and inconsistent reformism. Only those patriotic radicals like J. A. Roebuck joined Palmerston in waving the Union Jack in the face of autocratic regimes.

Palmerston's tendency to carve out a constituency among the people seemed to befit the unpredictable state of political parties. Divisive forces were latently evident in both major parties even in the 1830s. Canning's death in 1827 revealed a fault-line in Tory ranks which was not easily mended by Peel's victory in 1841. Nor did making the Whigs the butt of Tory criticism rally the nation behind the new prime minister. Rather, Peel saw that in assembling his ministry, he had to respond innovatively to the public's call for change, most notably the repeal of the Corn Laws. By the end of the Melbourne ministry, the demand for changes in the Corn Laws was difficult to ignore. In a last-minute effort to attract free traders to the Whig side without raising taxes, Lord John Russell was ready to accept a fixed duty on grain. Encouraged by the Whigs' action, the Anti-Corn League stepped up their efforts to broadcast their message to the nation. Then when it was seen as a message that appealed across party lines, Peel considered it as fair game for adoption when he took office in August 1841. His remedy was to stimulate trade by introducing a reduction of the sliding scale on corn. In 1842 and 1845, Peel worried his agrarian supporters by further reducing the duties on corn. By late 1845, Peel realized that the movement in the direction of Corn Law reform and a full-blown free-trade policy was inevitable despite the political consequence of breaking up his party. Inspired by their rising star, Benjamin Disraeli, this was enough for the Tory Protectionists to abandon Peel.[2]

While there were signs that divisions threatened party unity, there was no hint that Palmerston was about to bolt his Whig colleagues. If anything, the threat of a no-confidence motion against the Whigs in 1841 strengthened his commitment to them. Palmerston urged Melbourne to go to the people in a national election rather than resign in the face of parliamentary defeats.[3] In campaigning at Tiverton in 1841, Palmerston never wavered in his enthusiastic support for Whig-sponsored reforms such as the New Poor Law and abolition of slavery. Foreseeing the coming battle over the Corn Laws, he urged his constituents to oppose protectionism and favour Russell's free trade bill. Even when the Tory victory forced the Whigs into opposition, there was no indication that Palmerston would abandon them. In fact, when he was safely returned for Tiverton, he was impatient for an opportunity to undo the Tories' foreign policy by returning to the Foreign Office in a revived Whig Cabinet.[4]

Few issues so clearly distinguished Palmerston from the Tories as the management of Anglo-French relations. When the two nations had come close to war during the Mehemet Ali crisis, Palmerston had done little to relieve the tension between them. Driven by his heightened sense of national self-interest, Palmerston bristled whenever he saw Britain subjected to French exploitation. He saw this in a squabble between Catholic priests and Protestant missionaries in Tahiti and when both nations jostled with each other to control events in Spain or Portugal. Fearful that the sensitive balance of power in Europe be upset, especially by a France whose people longed for a revival of *le gloire*, Palmerston guarded against any softening of British policy.[5]

Palmerston had further distinguished himself from the Tories by consistently attacking Aberdeen's friendly relations with the Americans. This was not the first time that Palmerston had found himself at odds with the American government. Ever since the war of 1812, he had grown more and more uneasy about this fledgling country's growth as a nation. While he and the Whigs were moderate reformers, it seemed as if the Americans were plunging headlong in the direction of universal suffrage, as exemplified by the election of Andrew Jackson in 1828. However, Palmerston's deeper concern focused on the Americans' intentions towards Canada. Border disputes remained unresolved since the 1783 Treaty of Paris which ended the American War of Independence. In 1828, an arbitration agreement gave the state of Maine more land at the expense of the province of Nova Scotia. The situation worsened, however, when the boundary dispute extended westward into the vicinity of the Great Lakes and the Rocky Mountains. When Lord Ashburton, representing Lord Aberdeen, negotiated a final settlement of the US–Canadian border dispute with the Secretary of State, Daniel Webster, Palmerston leaped to the attack. Using his influence at the *Morning Chronicle*, he tried to turn public opinion against the agreement.[6] When the House of Commons soundly condemned Palmerston's position, there was a general feeling that he had misread the public's desire for peace.[7] Clearly, Palmerston's reputation for taking a hard line in foreign policy still preceded him and set him apart from more circumspect politicians.

Although Palmerston's foreign policy views had become predictable by now, he continued to redefine himself in domestic affairs. If Palmerston had been a Canningite in his apprentice years, as time went on he became a liberal, even a radical, in his response to pressing grievances. Apart from a general sense of *noblesse oblige*, Palmerston was not a man of abstract principles, driven philosophically to assist the downtrodden. In fact, it would be more accurate to say that his eighteenth-century aristocratic upbringing inclined him to accept impoverishment and misery as part of the natural order of things. The origin of Palmerston's sensitivity to humanitarian causes can be traced to his step-son-in-law, Lord Anthony Ashley, later the 7th Earl of Shaftsbury. Palmerston's step-daughter Minnie Cowper was married to Ashley, the Tory evangelical, whose factory reforms improved the wretched lives of women and children. Although Ashley had his critics on the right and left,

Palmerston was sympathetic to some of his step-son-in law's ideas. For example, in 1842 he spoke in support of Ashley's bill ending the employment of women and children in coalmines.[8] Unlike Ashley, however, he was not driven by higher motives but by the practical fact that children belonged in schools, not in mines. Otherwise, he asked, how could they expect the working class to be morally upright unless they are properly educated? He also voted for the 1844 Ten Hours Bill which limited the daily hours of labour for women and men under eighteen. Although Palmerston's support for such measures could not always be taken for granted, on this issue he was even open to the lobbying pressures from Chartists and their humanitarian arguments.[9]

Palmerston also outpaced many of his Whig colleagues in making repeated demands for the enforcement of the anti-slave trade laws. From the time that Britain committed itself in 1815 to enforce the abolition of the slave trade under the terms of the Congress of Vienna, it was a major goal of his foreign policy. For example, he chastised France and the United States, in particular, for their slowness in executing the law. However, from time to time, he appeared to break ranks with abolitionists, specifically the Anti-Slavery Society which favoured slavery's total abolition. Palmerston, ever the pragmatist, believed that abolition was achievable, but also realized that men of property would oppose any challenge to their rights.[10] In 1845 this may have been the wily politician speaking. More likely, however, it was Palmerston the aristocrat, sensitive to his own property interests, although he himself never owned slaves.

In Ireland, Palmerston's reformist inclinations were, at best, uneven. He had from the beginning been open to Catholic Emancipation or some other remedy for the political and legal inequalities suffered by Irish Catholics. Like some Whigs, he believed that giving Irish Catholics access to the political process would provide solutions to their economic and social grievances. There were, however, distinct limits to how far he would go. He opposed repeal of the Act of Union or any form of home rule. On the other hand, while he was a champion of order, he was reluctant to use heavy-handed coercion to calm Irish discontents. He was also uneasy about rack-renting and the use of arbitrary evictions. Instead, he admonished landlords to be compassionate, as he himself tried to be on his Sligo estates. Such sympathy, however, always stopped short of invading the landlord's property rights. It is fair to say that Palmerston's public and private stances on Irish matters was consistent but cautious. As an Irish landlord, he maintained an arm's-length relationship with his tenants, striving paternalistically to make improvements in his estates but ideologically unable to cross a line that might be at odds with his own interests.

Few events tested his good will towards the Irish more than the devastating potato famine that began in 1845. As the principal landlord in County Sligo, he was intimately acquainted with the destitution and death visited upon the people.[11] Palmerston's initial response to the famine testified to his inability to adjust his free market mentality to the economic and social needs of the burgeoning Irish population. Any attempt by the British government to supply grain to the starving Irish, he argued, would put private merchants out of business while imposing more burdens on the taxpayer. Instead, he shifted the blame to the Irish people for over-populating the country.[12] In general, Palmerston seemed detached from, and bemused by, the plight of the Irish. The bleak reports of famine-related deaths, unemployment and the failure of public works projects, seemed to have left him unmoved. He did provide a small amount of corn meal and some employment, but little more.[13]

The best he could do was to subsidize his tenants' emigration to North America. Compared with other landlords, Palmerston's contribution to the emigrants was considered fairly generous. In 1847, he and other landlords sent nine ships from Sligo to Canada, carrying some 2000 tenants. When they arrived at St John, New Brunswick, there were horrific reports suggesting that Palmerston had left his tenants ill-equipped to deal with the journey. Newspapers in Quebec and St John told shocking tales of naked and starving women and children. However, it is doubtful that Palmerston was involved directly in this emigration process. Rather, it is more likely that he left this task to his estate agents.

On the face of it, Palmerston's distant and seemingly indifferent approach to the crisis in Ireland appears inconsistent with his reputation for championing liberal causes abroad. When understood in a larger context, however, a different picture of the man emerges. Palmerston was struggling to reconcile government intervention in Ireland with his own developing notions of a free market society. Indeed, when news came from his estate agents that his costs for food and poor relief would increase indefinitely as the famine worsened, he reaffirmed his *laissez-faire* position. Opposition to a social welfare solution, however, did not mean he had forsaken his impoverished tenants. The decision to provide the alternative of assisted emigration seemed to be a better solution for himself and his destitute tenants. For Palmerston, it meant subsidizing his tenants' flight from poverty in exchange for reduced poor rates and the estates' recouped property value. Moreover, his treatment of emigrant tenants should be seen in the light of certain circumstances. The condition of the emigrants prior to their departure may or may not have been under the control of Palmerston and his agents. If, for example, the tenants were too ill-clothed to withstand the rigours of the sea voyage, perhaps that was became of their destitute condition in 1847. Moreover, criticism of Palmerston must be balanced with passengers' testimony commending him for his well-intentioned effort to help them emigrate. Overall, it should be understood that in facing the challenge of the Irish Famine Palmerston, like many other politicians in the mid-nineteenth century, was constantly having to review and change his policy. As he adjusted his principles to meet the necessities of the day, he lacked the knowledge and experience to make fully informed public policy decisions. He had been willing to experiment with reforms, such as factory act legislation, but the Irish Famine and all the allied problems associated with land tenure were so intractable that he lacked any ready solution.[14]

When Britain's political world was shaken in 1846 by the split in the Tory party, Palmerston's influence on the new alignment of men and measures became pivotal. It remained to be seen what part Palmerston would play in any political re-alignment, but the Tory split created a new context in which he could operate. Given Peel's inability to govern, the Queen, in desperation, turned to Lord John Russell to a form a new Whig ministry. Russell was not blind to Palmerston's growing popularity in the country and knew that he needed him in the Cabinet. A minority of Whigs opposed his re-appointment but the great majority welcomed him back. His Whig party credentials had passed the test and his return to the Foreign Office was secure.[15]

When Palmerston re-entered the government in 1846, Anglo-French tensions again commanded his attention. He had endeavoured to improve his personal ties with France while in Opposition by visiting Paris, accompanied by Lady Palmerston. When meeting with his former antagonists, Thiers, Guizot and the writers Alexander Dumas and Victor Hugo, he was all Palmerston – buoyant, magnanimous and utterly charming.[16] So friendly had this relationship become that Palmerston began calling it an *entente cordiale*.[17] However, no matter how warm these friendly meetings appeared on the surface, they could not dispel Palmerston's deep-seated suspicions formed in his early years at the

Foreign Office. In many respects, the fragile Quadruple Alliance of 1834 (between Britain, France, Spain and Portugal) had been more honoured in the breach. From Britain's standpoint, the agreement succeeded because it kept France from embracing the Eastern Powers and prevented Austria, Russia and Prussia from meddling in Iberian affairs. It did not, however, keep Palmerston from being suspicious of French intentions in trying to maintain stable regimes in Madrid or Lisbon.

In 1846, he seized an opportunity to test Anglo-French amity when the Spanish queen mother, Maria Christina, began making marriage preparations for her sixteen-year-old daughter, Isabella, and her sister, the Infanta Luisa. As soon as the names of potential candidates were broached, it caught the diplomats' attention. Firstly, under the Treaty of Utrecht of 1713, France and Spain were prohibited from contracting any diplomatic marriages that allowed for a merger of the two thrones. Secondly, during the Spanish Civil War of the 1830s, Palmerston had supported a radical faction known as the Exaltados, fearful that a more right-wing group favoured by the French and the queen mother might gain the upper hand. On the one hand, these precautions were quite consistent with the Quadruple Alliance of 1834, which brought France and Britain together as protectors of Spain and Portugal against intervention by the Eastern Powers. On the other hand, it also allowed Palmerston to keep his eye on French machinations in the Iberian Peninsula.

In 1843, a right-wing group favoured by the queen mother and the French overthrew the Exaltados. Although Palmerston blamed Aberdeen for ceding this advantage to the French in Madrid, the change did not affect the marriage issue. In an effort to preclude such talk, in 1845 Aberdeen and Guizot verbally agreed to disavow any Anglo-French claims to the hand of the Spanish princesses. Instead, the marital candidates were to be restricted to Isabella's cousins, the Duke of Cadiz and the Duke of Seville. The matter seemed settled, but loose talk at the court of Madrid kept alive other marital expectations, which, in turn, threatened the *entente cordiale*. Aberdeen had persisted in dampening such rumours, but when Palmerston returned to the Foreign Office in 1846 he further complicated matters. In a dispatch to Henry Lytton Bulwer, the British ambassador in Madrid, he wrote that the British government would not interfere in the Spanish marriage affair unless the choice was seen as upsetting the balance of power. Since the 1845 agreement had excluded Louis-Philippe's heirs from consideration, Palmerston said that he was open to other candidates including the two Spanish dukes and Leopold of Saxe-Coburg, Queen Victoria's first cousin. Although he had stipulated that the dispatch was confidential, on the following day, 20 July, Palmerston revealed its contents to the French chargé d'affaires, and in an effort to improve relations with France, invited him to show the contents to Guizot.[18] Predictably, the French, goaded by the conniving Princess Lieven (Guizot's current mistress), seized the opportunity to score a diplomatic victory over Britain and Palmerston. Before Palmerston could react, it was announced on 4 September 1846, that Queen Isabella would marry a Spanish duke but, contrary to the 1845 agreement, Luisa would wed the Duke of Montpensier, a son of Louis-Philippe. The British unsuccessfully argued that such a marriage was in violation of the Treaty of Utrecht. It could be argued that these marriages mattered little diplomatically. As it happened, the birth of a son to Queen Isabella precluded Princess Luisa from making any claim to the throne, and so there was no danger of French encroachment on the Spanish government. However, the important point in this episode is that just as Palmerston was about to launch his second term at the Foreign Office, he suffered a diplomatic setback.

It appears that Palmerston, with uncharacteristic *naïveté*, had allowed the French to enjoy a diplomatic coup at the expense of Britain. But in sharing his confidence with the French he seemed to know exactly what he was doing, namely that there was a benefit to be gained but not without risk. In this case, the benefit was the continuance of Aberdeen's policy of improving Anglo-French relations for the sake of peace and stability in Europe. It is clear from his dispatch of 19 July that Palmerston was open to any number of marriage arrangements, short of a union with the French royal family. This flexibility suggests that, despite his dislike of queen mother Maria Christina's regime and the disappearance of true constitutionalism in Spain, he wanted to avoid forceful intervention. Also, he did not want to jeopardize the fragile Quadruple Alliance by heightening tensions with the French and thereby driving Guizot into the arms of the Eastern Powers. His critics in Parliament and at Court could have demanded more from Palmerston but in the end decided against this. Outrage from Tories, Victoria and Albert, and the public generally was so directed at the French government that Palmerston's blunder paled in comparison. Moreover, it turned out to be a hollow victory for Guizot for in less than two years Louis-Philippe would be driven into exile, leaving the future status of the *entente cordiale* in doubt.

Meanwhile, Palmerstonianism was further tested in Portugal in 1845 when the radical Septembrists had revolted against Queen Maria da Gloria. Palmerston was caught between remaining committed to protecting Queen Maria da Gloria's regime or being sympathetic to the Septembrist rebels. Bowing to pressure from Queen Victoria to go to Maria's defence, Palmerston reluctantly sent ships to Oporto to dislodge the Septembrists while also pleading for clemency on their behalf. In trying to please Victoria, he roused the anger of English parliamentary radicals annoyed at his apparent abandonment of the Septembrists. In the end, Palmerston managed to please almost everyone. On the one hand, he quieted Victoria and Albert's concerns by using force to safeguard the Portuguese queen's place on the throne. On the other, in gaining pardons for the Septembrist rebels, he enhanced his standing with the English radicals.[19]

Palmerston acted similarly in responding to Austria's attempt to take over the independent Republic of Cracow in 1846, after its people had risen in sympathy with Polish rebels. He protested to Austria and its ally Prussia that their actions violated the Congress of Vienna, but he refused Guizot's invitation to act against them. At first glance, it appeared that Palmerston had allowed the Eastern Powers to take advantage of Britain's growing estrangement from France. Undoubtedly, revenge for Guizot's victory over the Spanish marriages cannot be ignored, but other factors seem to have dictated Palmerston's action in Cracow. Firstly, always the realist, he knew that Britain could do little to help the Polish dissidents in a remote, land-locked area. Secondly, 1846 was hardly an auspicious time to encourage French radicals to foment a European war over the Polish cause. Moreover, heroic action was unnecessary when a wrist-slapping warning to the Austrians sufficed to strengthen his reputation in Europe as a friend of liberalism.

As revolutionary dissent surfaced throughout Europe, climaxing in the *annus mirabilis* of 1848, Palmerston's liberal credentials were further challenged at home and abroad. While he was fast becoming the darling of radicals who praised his international liberalism, a different Palmerston was responding to domestic crises. When the country girded itself for the announced Chartist demonstration on Kennington Green on 10 April 1848, he showed that he was no friendlier to the Chartists than to violent revolutionaries abroad. At the time, Palmerston relished the opportunity to command a contingent of men in defending the Foreign Office. He had always been an advocate of order, especially when riot and revolution threatened property. At Peterloo in 1819, the Newport Rising of 1839 or with the more recent threats from the Chartists, Palmerston consistently chose coercion over conciliation. At the same time, he was able to defend basic human and political rights in the House of Commons, especially when they were being fought for in distant lands. In responding to charges levelled at him by the Chartist leader George Julian Harney in the 1847 Tiverton election campaign, Palmerston demonstrated skill in dodging the accusation that he was a false liberal. Harney tried to link him to the government's draconian Six Acts of 1819, a Chinese foreign policy that sponsored the sale of opium, and support for a reactionary Turkish sultan. In a long, comprehensive rebuttal, mixing half-truths with generalizations, Palmerston adroitly captured the support of the crowd. The gloss he placed over his conduct brought cheers from people already inclined to favour him. In supporting the use of coercion, he answered that he generally favoured persuasion over force, and in defending his accomplishments abroad he characterized his interventions in places such as the Middle East and Portugal as victories for peace and stability.[20] His performance was a *tour de force*. Humorous by turns, upbeat and completely in control of the facts, albeit twisted to suit his purposes, it was a classic Palmerston stump speech geared to the mood of the crowd and well covered by a congenial press corps.

To compare Palmerston's liberal credentials at home with his advocacy of constitutionalism abroad, in a sense, misses the point. The liberal goals that he heralded abroad, such as fundamental human rights and freedom from arbitrary rule, were not those being demanded by the Chartists – they wanted universal suffrage, a secret ballot and salaries for Members of Parliament. His readiness to use British intervention to safeguard constitutional regimes made sense to Palmerston only because it served British interests in maintaining the balance of power.[21] Revolution, after all, could also invite intervention by outside powers that would upset the balance of power. In Spain and Portugal there was the immediate prospect of France opportunistically taking advantage of unstable situations. The Eastern Powers posed less of a real danger in Iberia due mainly to the 1834 Quadruple Alliance. Still, any crisis, especially a local one, occurring in near proximity to the Eastern Powers, ran the risk of a regional conflict quickly becoming an international incident.

On the eve of the 1848 revolutions, a minor incident of this sort occurred in Switzerland as chronic tensions between Catholic and

Protestant cantons threatened to spiral into a civil war. Fearful that the Protestant cantons would alter the constitution of the Swiss Confederation, the Catholic minority united defensively into an alliance known as the Sonderbund. When the Federal Diet, led by the Protestant cantons, declared this action illegal, civil war followed. As expected, the conservative powers, led by Metternich, supported the Sonderbund. Guizot, who was cultivating new ties with the east as an alternative to his dependency on Britain, also offered French support to the Catholics.

The parallel between events in Cracow in 1846 and Switzerland in 1847 seemed plain enough to Palmerston. He could not afford to stand by as conservative forces rallied to buttress the endangered minority of Catholic cantons. Against this array, Palmerston was in a position to act forcefully. Instead, he tried to throw the French and Austrians off balance by proposing that an international conference be convened. He also sent his friend Sir Gilbert Elliott, the 2nd Earl of Minto, on missions to Berne and Rome in the autumn of 1847. Elliott counselled the Protestant radicals in Berne to be patient in dealing with the Sonderbund and to wait for negotiations to work. However, Guizot attributed more sinister motives to the visit, particularly when shortly afterwards the Protestant forces attacked the Catholic canton of Fribourg, effectively defeating the Sonderbund alliance. Despite Palmerston's denials, the conservative press leapt to attack him for this incident. The English radicals, including the liberal newspapers, took their cue from these attacks upon Palmerston by championing him as the agent of freedom in Europe. Whether or not Palmerston had instigated the violence in Fribourg, the European conservatives had invented him as a larger-than-life force in European politics, while his friends in the English press did their part to cultivate the growth of this popular myth.[22]

It might be said that Palmerston inadvertently won a diplomatic victory in Switzerland if measured by France and Austria's failure to protect the Sonderbund from the Swiss radicals. Similarly, Guizot's shortlived courtship of Metternich did not cause a permanent re-alignment of diplomatic relationships. If one believes that Palmerston played a role in the radicals' conquest of Catholic Fribourg, then it could be argued that he presented the French and the Austrians with a *fait accompli* from which they could not recover. By 1848, the revolutionary impulses already felt in Switzerland and Italy would overtake all of Europe, forcing the Eastern Powers to turn their attention to their own domestic crises. One can only speculate that without revolutionary distractions at home, a conservative counter-attack would have prevailed over the Swiss radicals.

Although the conservatives had linked Palmerston's name to the liberal cause in Switzerland, it would be wrong to associate him with the revolutionary movements emerging in Italy. Palmerston's goal in Switzerland had been to foster liberal change but to do so without provoking intervention by the Eastern Powers. Such intervention would have had the effect of transforming a local contest into an international war.[23] Having just averted a crisis in Switzerland, Palmerston was equally keen to avoid another one in Italy. Elliot's next mission, to the Pope, was aimed at sponsoring constitutionalism as an alternative to revolution. Pius IX had already shown his reformist colours when he ascended the papal throne in 1846. Elliot's task was to urge the Pope to stay on this reformist course despite the revolutionary rumblings in the Papal States. In the spring of 1847, demonstrations occurred in Austrian-controlled Lombardy and Venetia. Austrian troops occupied Ferrara and were poised to attack King Charles Albert of Sardinia if he granted a constitution to his people in Piedmont. Palmerston realized that Austrian intervention would invite a French response with the prospect of war to follow. Perhaps Britain could have played a more intrusive role in Italy as a supporter of liberalism and progress. Palmerston thought of sending the fleet to Civitavecchia on Italy's west coast as a warning to Metternich not to use reform efforts as a pretext for committing territorial aggression.[24] However, Palmerston was wise enough to know that specific threats should be avoided lest one is forced to carry them out.

The events of 1848, however, which saw the creation of a new French republic, the collapse of the Metternichian system, and movements for unification in Germany and Italy, were to transform Palmerston's thinking. The series of revolutions which erupted in 1848 had their origin in the 1789 French Revolution. Although the Great Powers had driven the principles born of that revolution underground in 1815, they surfaced again throughout Europe in popular movements for political and economic reforms. In the period between 1815 and 1848, the struggles for liberalism and nationalism demonstrated that the 1789 principles were still alive. Ultimately, these persistent impulses for reform, when left unfulfilled, were to pave the way for the violent upheavals of 1848.

When the French Revolution broke out in Paris on 23 February 1848, it produced a broad-based republican government, which kept socialist and extremist elements at bay. Despite some criticism from Queen Victoria, Palmerston accepted the new regime with equanimity and gave it unofficial approval.[25] He was not enamoured of republicanism and believed that by granting universal suffrage, the French 'will set our non-voting population agog, and will create a demand for an inconvenient extension of the suffrage, ballot, and other mischievous things.' Also, he thought that in general the French republic was capable of being 'inherently aggressive'.[26] Such aggression would only elicit hostile responses from conservative European powers, he thought. The republican solution, however, was the best that Britain could hope for if they wished to prevent a proletarian takeover. Arguing that the reaction might be worse than the revolution itself, he sent a cautionary signal to Russia, Prussia and Austria, asking them to accept the new French government.[27] Even the startling announcement by the new French leader, Alphonse de Lamartine, that France would no longer recognize the provisions of the Congress of Vienna left Palmerston unperturbed. He realized that this was merely revolutionary rhetoric and not a prescription for territorial aggrandizement.

Although Palmerston's policy towards the French provisional government was cautiously supportive, he was sensitive to the alarms raised by Louis Blanc's use of National Workshops and the plan to nationalize the French railway system. Not surprisingly, Palmerston welcomed the return of order in June 1848, when General Louis Cavaignac's military rule replaced Lamartine even though some 10,000 lives were lost in the mêlée.[28] He did show leniency towards individual exiles, such as Louis Blanc, but clearly the events in France had helped to clarify his views about the menace of revolution. Still, the return of a Bonaparte to rule in France did not seem to alarm Palmerston. However, the election of Louis Napoleon, nephew of the great Napoleon, as the new president of the Second Republic in December 1848 caused a stir in most European capitals. Palmerston had kept abreast of the fast-moving changes occurring in French politics, but in late 1848 his mind was still preoccupied by the need for peace in Italy. If he still hoped to follow a policy of cooperative restraint, involving joint action by Britain and France in Lombardy and Venetia, then cordial relations with the French government, despite its changing incarnations, was required.

When Palmerston realized that the simple granting of constitutional reforms was not enough to satisfy the revolutionaries, he began to approach each uprising cautiously. For example, when Metternich's flight from Austria in March 1848 accelerated Italian unification efforts, Palmerston, always suspicious of Italian nationalism, feared that the movement would fall into radical hands. He also realized that a weakened Austria would no longer be a stabilizing force against Tsarist ambitions or uncontrolled nationalism in Germany.[29] Once the revolution had occurred in France, he was concerned that Austria's weakness would tempt the French to exploit the situation in Lombardy–Venetia. Accordingly, he advised the new government in Vienna to cut their losses by surrendering Lombardy to Sardinia, otherwise Charles Albert and the French would take it by conquest. Under Palmerston's plan, the Austrian Emperor would retain control of Venetia but only if he granted constitutional reforms to its people.

However, before Palmerston could complete these negotiations, the aged Austrian commander Field Marshal Radetzky revived the Austrian cause with a series of military victories over Charles Albert. Palmerston tried to regain the initiative by proposing Anglo-French mediation. A delayed response from Austria permitted Radetzky and his brutish henchman General Haynau to ravage the Italian people with their atrocities. Palmerston was enraged by this barbarity but the events in northern Italy were now beyond his control. It did not help that Queen Victoria had favoured the Austrian counter-offensive.[30] All that Palmerston could do was resort to a fusillade of protests, condemning Radetzky's conduct.

The situation then worsened when Guiseppi Garibaldi, the leader of the revolutionary Red Shirts, proclaimed the Roman Republic, forcing the Pope to flee the Holy City in November 1848. This erstwhile reform-minded pope, recoiling at liberalism's violent face, called for help from Europe's Catholic sovereigns. At this point, Palmerston disliked the choices facing him. On the one hand, he did not approve of Garibaldi's victory and the precedent set by establishing a revolutionary republic in Rome. On the other hand, the convergence of Austrian and French military forces on Italy was also unwelcome. Palmerston preferred that Britain play a diplomatic role by ensuring the Pope's independence or having Charles Albert intervene.[31] Palmerston's advice, however, went unheeded by all the parties. Louis Napoleon, France's new president, eventually defeated the Republican forces in Rome and restored Pius IX to the papal throne. Charles Albert, against Palmerston's advice, renewed hostilities with the Austrians and was again routed by Radetzky's troops. Choosing exile, he abdicated in favour of his son, Victor Emmanuel. Finally, counter-revolutions came to Sicily in the summer of 1848, when King Ferdinand of Naples brutally suppressed the rebels. Palmerston had advised the Sicilians to settle for constitutional guarantees but they had gambled on a complete break with the past, and lost.

Palmerston's acceptance of revolutionary change in Italy was, at best, lukewarm. His support for domestic improvements including constitutional limits on arbitrary rule and modernizing changes never ran to extremes. Therefore, short-lived victories for liberal nationalism could hardly be seen as Palmerstonian successes. His advocacy of change was always balanced by his desire for peace, a sentiment he shared with the Austrians. Similarly, his fear of French intervention in Piedmont was never so great that he envisioned using British force against it. Curiously, Palmerston once again was to benefit from popular sentiment when the counter-revolutionary forces succeeded. His public declarations against Radetzky's cruelties made him a friend to the radicals even if he had only reluctantly courted their affections.

Palmerston's response to the revolutionary movements in Italy and France was more complicated than his mere advocacy of constitutional reform. Metternich and his successors were obsessed with the image of Palmerston as the *agent provocateur* behind the revolutionary contagion sweeping through Europe. Ironically, revolutionary nationalists who felt betrayed by him in central Europe suffered from the same misreading of his intentions. The Hungarian Louis Kossuth was repeatedly rebuffed in seeking Palmerston's support for Magyar independence. He was told that revolution in Eastern Europe would only invite Russian intervention and jeopardize peace in the region.[32] When, in 1848, Palmerston said 'The Austrian Empire was worth saving', he meant that he did not want her so weakened that she would become dependent on Russia for assistance.[33] If the oft-quoted statement 'If the Austrian Empire did not exist, it would have to be invented' can be attributed to Palmerston, it is because he saw the Hapsburg Empire as the only political entity that could safeguard the states of Eastern Europe from internal fragmentation and outside exploitation.[34] This did not stop him from being sympathetic towards Hungarian refugees but he was able to say in his definitive speech of 21 July 1849,

> Austria is a most important element in the balance of European power. Austria stands in the centre of Europe, a barrier against encroachment on the one side, and against invasion on the other. The political independence and liberties of Europe are bound up, in my opinion, with the maintenance and

integrity of Austria as a great European Power; and therefore anything which tends by direct, or even remote, contingency, to weaken and cripple Austria...must be a great calamity to Europe, and one which every Englishman ought to deprecate, and to try to prevent.[35]

He also reasoned that if the Hungarians were crushed, then Austria would have destroyed part of its own empire and thereby weakened her role in maintaining the balance of power in Europe. In 1848, Palmerston had urged Austria to rid itself of Lombardy, because its severance would ultimately strengthen the Empire. The loss of Hungary, on the other hand, would so destabilize the Hapsburg estates that Austria would no longer serve as the centre of gravity around which the 1815 Vienna settlement revolved. Although he had been called intemperate in his defence of constitutionalism in other countries, when Palmerston found himself in the uncertain waters of liberal nationalism in central Europe, he cautiously anchored himself to the Congress system, with Austria as its guarantor. Fearful of Russia and Prussia acting as Austria's replacement in Germany and the Balkans, he chose the short-term recourse of defending the status quo.

In contrast, Palmerston should have invited a change to the status quo in Germany in 1848.[36] While he may have found that the forces of nationalism were troubling and unpredictable, he had every reason to support the German liberals' call for a united Germany when they assembled in Frankfurt. A united Germany would be a sentinel against French territorial ambitions in the Rhineland as well as an obstacle to Russian incursions from the east. A new Germany led by liberals could join Britain and France in supporting Polish nationalism against Russian repression. A new Germany, unlike the older confederation with its protectionist *Zollverein*, also offered the prospect of being a rich trading partner with Britain. However, in the context of 1848, as nations girded themselves against the revolutionary storms, Palmerston was not ready to countenance important territorial arrangements that might undermine the Vienna settlement. The test case came with the liberal proposal to incorporate the duchies of Schleswig and Holstein into a larger Germany. The Danish king had traditionally ruled both duchies but in 1815 Christian VII allowed Holstein, with its predominantly ethnic German population, to become part of the Germanic Confederation. The 1848 revolution broke up the union between Schleswig and Holstein, with the former staying within Denmark while the latter retained its position in the Confederation. This settlement pleased few people, least of all the inhabitants of the duchies and the Germans. Behind Palmerston's support for the status quo lay his fear of using ethnic principles to determine territorial sovereignty. If the German inhabitants of Holstein possessed such rights then might not Alsace be separated from France on the same basis?

Palmerston's response to the Schleswig–Holstein question was further complicated by Prussia's role in central Europe after Metternich's fall from power. As the revolutionary spirit spread to Germany, Palmerston found Prussia's new assertion of leadership to be disturbing. Although he welcomed Prussia's good offices being used to stay Austria's hand against Sardinia, he was troubled when King Frederick William supported a French plan to free Poland from Russian control. This suggested that Berlin had become enthralled in the revolutionary spirit of the March days. Although at first the plan looked impractical, from the Prussian standpoint it had the advantage of distracting the French from re-asserting their claims on the Rhineland. Palmerston responded cautiously but not complacently to these Prussian manoeuvres. In addition to his fear of Prussia being drawn into the French orbit were his concerns about the kaiser's assertion of power in Schleswig–Holstein. All these circumstances helped shape Palmerston's view of German liberalism, so that when Prussian liberal ministers began losing the initiative to the radicals in May and June, he increasingly distanced himself from the liberals' cause.

The German liberals, disappointed by Palmerston's opposition to their cause, lost whatever respect they originally had had for him. This response, however, suggests a serious misreading of his priorities at mid-century. While not abandoning constitutionalism in Germany, Palmerston did not want it at the risk of war. Fearful that the drive for German unification and liberalism would only end in war with Russia, he asked whether those in Frankfurt were bent on rushing 'into Conflict [sic] with all Europe, including, as it seems, Prussia'. If Palmerston had to accept the inevitability of unification, then he could no longer rely on the 1815 settlement to maintain peace and stability. It has been suggested that if the German liberals had advanced their programme for unification more cautiously, without frightening the British and the Russians with their territorial claims, they would have persuaded men like Palmerston that they were the proper successors to Metternich in central Europe.[37]

In producing a peaceful, albeit unpopular solution in Germany, Palmerston had salvaged something from the 1848 revolutions.

Ironically, in following a more moderate course, he found himself again at odds with the crown. Victoria and Albert, showing their kinship ties to Germany, favoured the Germans over the Danes. Victoria believed that Germans, unlike other peoples, were more advanced and thus better able to profit from constitutional freedoms. Palmerston, taking a page from the recent French experiment with republicanism, agreed that Germany was suited to having free institutions, but he questioned whether its people could maintain the proper balance between liberty and order.[38] To understand Victoria and Albert's position on Germany requires an appreciation of their depth of antagonism towards Palmerston's Italian policy. So certain were they that he was a passionate champion of Italian nationalism and liberalism at the expense of Austria that they believed he had played favourites in supporting Charles Albert's claim for territories in Venetia while denying the Germans access to Schleswig. With regard to Italy, Victoria and Albert ran to the defence of the Emperor's sovereign rights, while in Denmark they were ready to overlook the Danish king's dynastic claims. These petulant displays further illustrated Palmerston's deteriorating relations with the court and its misguided understanding of his diplomacy.

While these events may have led to Palmerston's dismissal in 1850, it proved impossible to turn him out in 1848. Palmerston survived the constant barrage of criticism coming from the throne throughout 1848 simply because Russell and most of the Cabinet supported him. Palmerston may have angered Victoria and Albert with his verbal assaults on Austria, his support for the Hungarian exiles or his propensity for sabre rattling, but Lord John Russell had little room to manoeuvre in dealing with an enormously popular foreign secretary. The Queen angrily concluded that Palmerston, now approaching his sixty-fourth year, was incorrigible and therefore should be dismissed. However, Russell was only sustained in office by a coalition of MPs whose differences with each other were greater than their opposition to the Whigs. Above this party division stood Palmerston whose increasing favour with the people made his presence in any government a prerequisite for survival. In that sense, the rickety Whig Cabinet still needed Palmerston. However, the events that were to follow challenged even that proposition.

If there was one event that illustrated Palmerston's influence on Britain's foreign policy and the manner in which it shaped the public mind, it was the crisis centring on the inconspicuous but shady character known as Don Pacifico. In the past, Palmerston had been ready run to the defence of a British subject in a foreign country, irrespective of its connection with larger diplomatic issues. Unpaid British creditors, English travellers endangered by a civil war in Spain or Portugal, or other British subjects victimized by an overzealous policeman, all had found a ready defender in Palmerston. While other great statesmen might have hesitated in assigning inordinate weight to such minor matters, Palmerston, as Lytton Bulwer tells us, 'had none of these scruples. Right, in his eyes, was right; and if he insisted upon it when a formidable enemy might be provoked, he treated with becoming scorn the argument that we should deal more gently with an inferior delinquent'.[39] In most instances, Palmerston's bullying demands were non-negotiable – English law took precedence over that of any foreign power where there was any doubt. He did not pursue groundless claims, but when there was some hint of legitimacy he doggedly pressed governments until they gave in, even if it meant using boycotts or bombardment. Typically, he selectively targeted vulnerable countries. Spain, Portugal and Greece, for example, were too weak to pose a threat to Britain and were accessible to the British navy. On the other hand, he used diplomatic protests against Russia, Austria and Prussia, but little more.

His use of gunboats to uphold the ordinary Englishman's rights as readily as he would enforce a treaty obligation, endeared Palmerston to the British public. Such intercessions on behalf of individuals, however, necessarily involved foreign governments and thereby complicated their relationship with Britain. No case so dramatized Palmerston's magnification of a single grievance into an international incident with domestic ramifications as that involving Don Pacifico. This Portuguese Jew, who claimed British citizenship because of his birth in Gibraltar, had been posted as Portugal's consul to Athens. Charges of forgery had cost him his position, but that did not keep him from rising high in the Greek–Jewish community. During an anti-semitic outburst in Athens in April 1847, a crowd vandalized and burned his home. Claiming that the Greek government had done little to protect him from these crimes, he sought redress from the British government. Despite his dubious claim, Palmerston took it up and pressed the Greek government for damages.[40]

This minor drama was played out against the larger backdrop of deteriorating Anglo-Greek relations that went back to 1829. Although an enthusiastic champion of Greek independence, Palmerston had not forgotten that its notoriously mismanaged government was steeply in arrears for overdue loans. Having already used the British navy successfully in the eastern Mediterranean in 1849 to defend Turkish interests despite objections from Russia and Austria, Palmerston knew that a similar military bluff might work against Greece. Predictably a flurry of protests came from Russia and France, co-guarantors with Britain of Greece's independence. Count Nesselrode, Russia's Chancellor, was annoyed that Britain had not given enough notice to the Russians, but Palmerston was unperturbed by such finger-wagging gestures. The bluff worked and by April 1850 British claims against the Greek government were settled and the private demands of Don Pacifico were satisfied.[41]

The next stage in the drama surrounding Don Pacifico then shifted to Parliament where on 17 June 1850 the House of Lords approved a vote of censure by 169 votes to 132 against Palmerston's conduct in Greece. The Tories, led by Lord Stanley, criticized Palmerston for his bullying tactics in using the questionable claims of a British subject to bring Britain to the brink of war.[42] In what seemed like a major setback, a turning point was reached in Palmerston's career. On 24 June, when J. A. Roebuck, a radical chauvinist, countered the Lord's vote with a resolution applauding Palmerston's management of foreign affairs, Palmerston was given the opportunity to defend himself. The next day, in a speech that lasted more than five hours, Palmerston spoke to a packed House of Commons. Known as his *Civis Romanus Sum* speech, Palmerston posed the fundamental question of whether the British government, as in days of ancient Rome, was ready to defend the rights of its people wherever they might be. He saw no reason why an ordinary Englishman, especially when caught in a foreign country which lacked the most basic constitutional guarantees, should not enjoy his ancient liberties. In a glorious rhetorical moment, he raised up mid-Victorian Britain as the model for mankind to follow while other nations still agonized over their recent revolutions.[43] The speech was greeted with prolonged and ecstatic cheering in House, and this continued long afterwards in the nation, especially among the respectable middle class whose ideals and aspirations Palmerston personified. He was later lionized at a Reform Club dinner where he spoke to some 750 people, filled with a sense of well-being and pride in being British. It neither mattered to his enthusiastic followers that his speech was filled with emotion more than reason and that it was a demagogic masterpiece. Nor was it immediately important that Lord John Russell and members of the Cabinet did not cheer as loudly as the radicals, whose members to a man supported Roebuck's resolution.

Even when sharper criticism was levelled at Palmerston, his popular standing still soared. When a rumour surfaced that he had been the target of a foreign conspiracy abetted by sniping domestic critics, this only further served to improve his reputation. The usual suspects included the gossipy Princess Lieven and Guizot, who were accused of floating gossip across the Channel. At home, his Tory opponents, the eccentric diarist Charles Grevelle and John Delane, the editor of *The Times* who helped to engineer the vote in the Lords against Palmerston, contributed to these rumours. What began as an attack on his foreign policy, depicting Palmerston as an international bully, quickly turned in his favour. Instead of being seen as some one who had isolated Britain as a pariah exploiting smaller nations, Palmerston was able to redeem himself as someone who was proud to speak for his nation. To use Russell's language, he was 'the Minister of England', defending its citizens against foreign repression.[44] In Palmerston, the British people thought that they found a protector of their ancient rights against those counter-revolutionary forces that ultimately prevailed in 1848.

While Palmerston had captured the imagination and favour of the British people in 1850, other forces gathered against him. At Court, Victoria and Albert's disenchantment with him had turned into bitter opposition. The Queen was outraged at the favour he had shown the Spanish radicals in 1846, and his benign response to the republican victory in France grated, as would any act that jeopardized the standing of legitimate monarchs facing revolutionary challenges in 1848. The Queen also felt insulted when Palmerston continually neglected to submit dispatches to her for her approval. This habit persisted long after it was first noted by Prince Albert and led to demands for Palmerston's dismissal from the Cabinet.[45]

Such royal pressure did not move Russell for he knew that his government relied on the liberal consensus that had rallied to Palmerston's side. New circumstances, however, dictated that something had to be done with Palmerston. Faced with dangers from the right and the left in France, Louis Napoleon, staged a coup on 2 December 1851, making himself Napoleon III of the Second Empire. Russell and the Whigs disapproved of the *coup d'état*, as did the Queen. Officially, the government assumed a neutral stance, but a year earlier Palmerston had confided to Lord Normanby that he sympathized with the French President in trying to deal with an unresponsive legislature.[46] What began as a private confidence became a *cause célèbre* leading to Palmerston's dismissal from the Cabinet. The incompatibility of the Cabinet's position and that of its Foreign Secretary was plain enough to Russell. Palmerston angrily rejected the offer of the Irish Lord Lieutenancy as a consolation prize and gave up the seals of office on 26 December. As expected, the liberal press was outraged and the radicals ran to his side. When Russell addressed the matter in Parliament, Palmerston's position seemed indefensible. It was bad enough that he had acted against the will of the Cabinet in favouring Napoleon's coup, but the situation had been made much worse when Russell made public a private memorandum of August 1850, revealing that Palmerston had persistently disobeyed Victoria in not showing her his diplomatic dispatches.[47]

But could Russell's ministry last without Palmerston? Its survival depended on a fragile alliance of parties who remained united only when they found issues to agree on. These groups were also capable of dividing over other measures. That prospect became a reality in February 1852, with Palmerston sitting in opposition. Russell moved the Militia Bill, calling for a scaled-down army that relied on the use of local militias. In response, Palmerston moved an amendment directly contradicting the bill's goals, by proposing a national army with a centralized administration. The amendment was passed by 13 votes. The Militia Bill failed and Russell resigned. Referred to by Palmerston as his 'tit-for-tat' with Russell, he had avenged his own dismissal of December 1851.[48] The Militia Bill's failure merely confirmed the fact that Russell and the Whigs no longer spoke for the nation. It would be doubtful that the new Tory ministry of Lord Derby, weakened by inexperience, could do any better. As the Queen tried to take the country in a new political direction, no party seemed able to command the public's attention. However, in capturing the British people's imagination in the Don Pacifico affair, Palmerston, unfettered by party ties, almost singlehandedly carried the nation with him. Ten years earlier, he had joined a Whig opposition confronted by challenges of reform at home and revolution abroad. Since 1841, the tumultuous events climaxing in 1848 further shaped his political evolution and prepared him for the future. His dismissal by Russell in 1851 was to set him free from the Whigs, ready to chart a new course released from party ties.

4

POLITICS WITHOUT PARTY

The Corn Law crisis of 1846 signalled a deep rift within the Tory party and a jostling for leadership among the Whigs. At the centre of this breakdown of ideological unity and party discipline was Palmerston. He had already captured the public's attention with his flamboyant foreign policy, independent mindedness and outspoken defence of British interests. By mid-century, it was obvious that he would play a central role as political parties struggled through the 1847 parliamentary elections, with neither the Whigs nor Tories enjoying working majorities in the House of Commons. The Tory numbers rose to 306 after the 1852 elections, but still fell short of a majority.[1] A sign of Palmerston's tactical influence was seen in the growing rivalry between himself and Lord John Russell for liberal opinion in Parliament and the country. Since becoming Prime Minister in 1846, Russell had been defending his Foreign Secretary from those who sought his dismissal, including the Queen and his detractors in the Cabinet. But he could do little else, knowing that without the popular Palmerston the ministry would fall. The Whigs had owed their political life to the split in the Tory opposition and to support from radicals and Irish nationalists. Russell, as leader of the Whigs, struggled to claim the leadership of this liberal phalanx, but it was Palmerston who had already won their hearts. Although the vote of confidence in the Don Pacifico affair had sustained the Whigs in office temporarily, there was no mistake that this was a victory for Palmerston and not for Russell's Cabinet. Nor could a victory be found in Palmerston's dismissal in December 1851, since it prefigured within weeks Russell's own end at the hands of Palmerston's 'tit-for-tat' motion defeating the Whigs' Militia Bill.

It might be said that when Palmerston left office in December 1851, he also left the Whig party. Certainly there was the prospect that he might rejoin the Tories as a member of Lord Derby's newly formed Cabinet in January 1852. As the likelihood of a Peelite–Protectionist reconciliation faded, so too did hope of Derby's minority government succeeding without help from others. It was not surprising, then, that a reluctant Palmerston was approached by Derby to serve as Chancellor of the Exchequer. The invitation itself was begrudging, particularly given the Court's icy relationship with Palmerston. Still, it had to be proffered, for it was better to have him in the Cabinet than act against them in opposition.[2] Palmerston's public silence in response to speculation about his plans was not indicative of his private thoughts. He considered the Exchequer, although he still longed for the Foreign Office which the Queen had placed beyond his reach. He did, however, aspire to be Prime Minister and considered himself a better candidate than either Russell or Derby. Short of getting an unlikely royal invitation to form a Cabinet, he wanted to prevent Russell from receiving one. He did not preclude the idea of Russell being in a new government, which he would join as an equal, but not under Lord John's leadership. He preferred that his Whig friend, the Marquess of Lansdowne, get the call, but his age and the suspicion that such an appointment would merely veil Palmerston's own ambition, made such a proposal unlikely.[3]

When Palmerston stood for re-election at Tiverton in July 1852, he had an opportunity to speak out on issues that might draw him closer to the Tories. Conspicuously absent from his speeches were references to free trade and yet it was known that his opposition to protectionism would prevent him from joining the Derby government. He reiterated his support for a strong national defence and his continuing opposition to parliamentary reform. Palmerston did not take the bait offered him by his Chartist critic Rowcliffe, when teased about opportunistically joining any ministry that would have him. Nor did the results of the election, which increased the Tory numbers in the House of Commons by 100, seem to sway Palmerston. Perhaps this was because Derby still led a minority government of 310, pitted against a conglomeration of 270 Whigs, 40 Peelites and 40 Irish nationalists.[4]

It was clear in private negotiations that free trade was not the issue clearing the way for Palmerston's reconciliation with the Tories. The over-riding question dealt more with men than measures, since it was an inescapable fact that the Derby government would not last without

Palmerston. Its inexperience and unfamiliarity to the public was comically revealed when the Cabinet's ministers were first announced in Parliament, moving the aged and deaf Wellington to shout 'Who? Who?' This sobriquet stuck to the ill-fated government, despite Derby's belief that so long as there was more division than unity in the Opposition, he could survive. This non-aggressive approach, called 'vigilant inactivity' by Angus Hawkins, worked in opposition when forming temporary alliances to defeat ministerial measures.[5] Incumbency, however, did not permit cautious, watchful waiting when the advancement of government measures always entailed the risk of failure. This risk appeared when Disraeli tried to substitute a higher income tax in his budget to replace repealed customs duties. In doing so, he found few allies and alienated many of the repentant Peelites who had been drifting back into the Tory camp. Peelites, inspired by Gladstone's blistering attack on the Disraeli effort, then joined Whigs in bringing down the Derby government. Amidst this internecine strife, Palmerston, who did not attend the budget debate, conveniently remained aloof but always available to join a new political alliance.

When Queen Victoria turned to the ageing Lord Aberdeen to form a coalition government composed of Peelites, Whigs and other liberals, this was a telling comment on the state of politics at mid-century. Despite their retreat from protectionism, the Tories still lacked strong leadership and were therefore unable to lead the country in a new direction. The choice of the Peelite Aberdeen over Russell signalled how far the latter had fallen from grace since his departure from the government one year earlier. Initially, Russell was offered the Foreign Office with some vague expectation that he might succeed Aberdeen as Prime Minister, but by February 1853 he reluctantly agreed to lead the House of Commons without a seat in the Cabinet. Sulking at Peelite pre-eminence on the front benches and wounded from his on-going jostling with Palmerston, Russell left the ministry in early 1855, more weakened than when he entered it.[6]

Some Whigs chafed at the disproportionate favour shown the Peelites, given their relatively few seats in the Commons. The Peelites captured six seats in the Cabinet, with William Gladstone as Chancellor of the Exchequer. Six Whigs held places in the Cabinet but few had prominent places. The Peelite bias testified to their lingering reverence for their posthumous leader, who had died prematurely in 1850, and to their sense of superiority as administrators. In the long term, this uneasy marriage of convenience prefigured the merger of Peelites,

Whigs and radicals into the modern Liberal Party, but from the outset the coalition was troubled by clashing ambitions and challenges to Aberdeen's enfeebled leadership.

Although the Aberdeen coalition could have been formed without Palmerston, it could not last without him. There were plenty of people urging him to accept invitations from Aberdeen. Entreaties came from Whigs (Clarendon and Lansdowne), Peelites (Gladstone) and even Lady Palmerston who was anxious about the family's financial resources.[7] The question was not whether he would return to office but in what capacity. Offers for the Admiralty were turned aside automatically. Ideally, he wanted the position of prime minister for he knew that he was a better man than Aberdeen. Yet, given his restless disposition, staying in 'political solitude'[8] was an unrealistic alternative. If he did nothing, he told his brother-in-law Laurence Sulivan, he would be accused of 'nourishing implacable personal resentments'. Joining the Derby government would, on the other hand, look like a 'reckless adventurer, without principles to restrain me, without friendships to care for, without character to lose'. Instead, as if forecasting the future, he asked, 'what would the great Liberal Party, not in the House of Commons, nor at Brooks, nor at the Reform Club, but in the United Kingdom, have said of such a course;…what would that party at Tiverton by whom I have so long been returned have said?'[9] Considerations of personal ambition and party loyalty aside, Palmerston saw himself responding to a higher call from the nation to seize the leadership of liberal public opinion.

This point has recently stirred fresh interest in the evolution of liberalism in the nineteenth century, and, in particular, Palmerston's influence upon it. In contrast to the received view that Palmerston was more of a hindrance than a help to the reform process, E. D. Steele gives us a politician who was not only the John Bull of constitutionalism abroad, but also the advocate of progressive change at home. Indeed, Steele argues that in eventually spearheading the organization of the modern Liberal Party, Palmerston ushered democracy into Britain.[10] Other historians remember Palmerston as the utterly pragmatic opportunist who did what he had to do to survive politically. Certainly, they would assert, he was no rival to Gladstone.[11] From another direction comes the view that Palmerston truly belonged to the people. Antony Taylor is not satisfied with the depiction of Palmerston as merely the champion of shopkeepers, a narrow body of merchants and manufacturers. Rather, he sees the working class flocking behind

Palmerston in the 1850s as his name became identified with the nation. Politics aside, Palmerston had already cut an attractive figure before the public as the flamboyant clubman and roguish womanizer. Rumours of his sexual prowess may have raised eyebrows at Court but the vulgar crowd relished them, especially as the subject of their bawdy ballads. The populace also preferred to see him as a friend to revolutionary refugees and an enemy to autocrats. As Palmerston's name became identified with the patriotic cause in the Crimea and the defence of the raj in India, his standing with the people spiralled upwards. Palmerston was also praised for his defence of such 1848 revolutionaries as Louis Kossuth.

Antony Taylor's thesis goes beyond E. D. Steele's reconfiguration of Palmerston as the father of modern democracy in Britain. While Steele's thesis is that Palmerston prepared the way for the work of later reformers – especially Gladstone – Taylor goes further in suggesting that the working classes were responding favourably to his message. Perhaps this tells us more about the radicals' adoption of Palmerston as a folk hero than it does about his investment in them. Drawing upon statements in radical journals, popular ballads and Chartist literature, Taylor discovers a groundswell of Palmerstonian support. This tells us about the people's claim on him but does it mean that he had a claim on them? Undoubtedly, Palmerston relished the crowd's applause but there is no evidence from him suggesting that he had made them his own. Rather, as Steele suggests, his rhetoric was aimed at the upper working class, whose aspirations made them more at home with the middle class than with the unrestrained lower orders. Taylor properly concludes that a new understanding of Palmerston's impact helps us to measure more accurately popular political participation at mid-century. It should also move historians to reconsider the broader dimensions of the fledgling Liberal Party and Palmerston's shaping of it.[12]

Palmerston's ascent to the Home Office in 1852 gave him the opportunity to reshape himself along reformist lines. Being Home Secretary also gave him pre-eminence on the front bench without being made responsible for challenging budget questions or tricky foreign policy issues.[13] Instead, he busied himself with advancing reforms to ameliorate the worsening after-effects of the Industrial Revolution. In August 1853, he introduced the Smoke Abatement Bill to deal with the increased air pollution that so characterized Britain's urban environment. Improvements were also made in the Factory Acts that further limited the hours of child labour. He also addressed workers' rights in preventing employers from paying wages in kind rather than in cash. Other compelling issues involving the public's welfare such as health and safety caught his attention. For example, he supported compulsory vaccination and he tried to stop the burial of the dead in churches. Although not abstemious, he also heeded the temperance advocates and put greater restrictions on alcoholic consumption.

A more revealing glimpse of Palmerston's efforts to mitigate human suffering is seen in his response to the call for penal reform. In dealing with the rise in crime, Palmerston found himself caught between those who demanded harsher deterrence and those penal reformers who called for a more merciful approach. To Palmerston, it seemed appropriate to distinguish between hardened criminals, who deserved long-term confinement, and those lesser offenders who deserved shorter sentences. Typically, at this time, incorrigible criminals and revolutionaries were transported to far-off Tasmania. There, good behaviour was rewarded with unsupervised work leaves, while the hardened convicts who did not mend their ways were severely disciplined. Penal reformers were unhappy with these sentencing schemes and pressed for greater changes. Meanwhile, transportation to colonial settlements predictably drew protests from local inhabitants who resented the presence of criminals in their midst. Palmerston's response to these pressures was the Penal Servitude Bill of August 1853, which ended transportation and placed criminals in British prisons with opportunities for leaves on good behaviour. The bill became law despite attempts to hobble it with amendments making its terms harsher.[14] Palmerston displayed the same reform-mindedness towards juvenile crime. Clearly influenced by Lord Shaftesbury, who had spearheaded changes in reform schools, Palmerston proposed the Reformatory Schools Bill of 1854 which allowed the transfer of boys from prisons to reform schools. He also had an abiding interest in improving the living conditions in these schools and the fate of students once they were released.[15]

Palmerston may have reinforced his standing with the radicals by using the Home Office for humanitarian causes, but he was also capable of alienating them as a spokesman for law and order. This meant employing the metropolitan police force to the fullest in keeping the threat of revolutionary violence, which had earlier swept through Europe, from visiting Britain. In 1853, Palmerston had to face radical criticism for restricting the freedom of the Hungarian revolutionary Louis Kossuth. Earlier, in 1848, Palmerston had been willing to suffer Victoria's sharp criticism for sympathizing with Kossuth as a refugee from Austrian repression. Five years later, Kossuth was implicated in a plot to manufacture weapons to assist Austrian rebels. *The Times*, no friend to Palmerston, broke the story, saying that Britain had become a sanctuary for foreign revolutionaries. As a reaction to this, Kossuth's radical sympathizers in Britain announced that he was a victim of a smear campaign. Caught in the crossfire of these claims, Palmerston refused to play into the radicals' hands by absolving Kossuth or prejudging him without a proper hearing.[16] Little came of this incident, but while it diminished Palmerston's standing among the radicals, it also gave him the opportunity to demonstrate to the public at large that he was as much a defender of order as he was of freedom. As he continued to cultivate his image away from Parliament, Palmerston realized that his growing support came not from some shrill radicals, but from a broader middle class inspired by the flattering articles in the *Morning Post*, the *Globe*, and the *Morning Chronicle*. The conservative *Times*, with its much greater circulation, may have been a formidable critic of Palmerston, but one cannot discount the influence of journals such as the *Post* in keeping him in the public eye, especially during the Crimean War.[17]

The mark left by Palmerston on the Aberdeen coalition can be measured less by his accomplishments as Home Secretary and more by his interference in the affairs of the Foreign Office. The Queen's acceptance of Palmerston in the coalition had been expressly contingent on his being excluded from the Foreign Office. When the coalition was formed in 1852, Lord John Russell became Foreign Secretary but, dissatisfied with that office, he reluctantly agreed to lead the House of Commons. George Villiers, 4th Earl of Clarendon, then filled his place at the Foreign Office. In fact, in an age marked by confusion in party politics and a lack of decisive leadership, no single person articulated the government's foreign policy. This state of uncertainty was compounded by pressures exerted by the shrill voice of public opinion as expressed in the sometimes irresponsible press. It was in this climate that Palmerston thrived, as someone who knew his mind and spoke it clearly, while others remained paralysed by uncertainty and frustration.

If Palmerston perceived any threat to Britain coming from Europe, it was from France and not from Russia. Although a defender of Napoleon III, he voiced concerns in 1852 that Britain was unprepared militarily to meet a threat from a France with expansionist designs.[18] As it turned out, Napoleon III's adventurism was directed eastward and not at Britain. Palmerston had foreseen this in 1851, when he warned the French not to test the Russians by threatening to protect Roman Catholic claims in the Holy Places. He knew that challenging Russia's guardianship of the Orthodox Christians in the Ottoman Empire pleased French Catholics and would be seen as a rebuff to the Tsar. Beyond the immediate quarrels over custody of the Holy Places, the French still viewed warily the Tsar's designs on the 'Sick man of Europe' and were ready to come to the Sultan' defence. Ever since the 1848 revolutions had been crushed, Russia had become the embodiment of all that was repressive. It did not seem to soften the Tsar's demonization or impede France's defence of the Sultan to know that the Ottoman Emperor was an autocrat.

The dispute over custody of the Holy Places was merely symptomatic of tensions that would explode in the Crimean War. Beginning with the Treaty of Kutchuk Kainardji of 1774, the Tsar had enjoyed a sphere of influence over the Ottoman Empire. According to the Straits Convention of 1841, the Russian right of protecting Constantinople, known as the Porte, had been replaced by the Great Powers guarantee of the status quo. Despite these modifications, the Tsar still hoped that Russia's expansionary dreams would be fulfilled once the dilapidated Turkish Empire had collapsed. Meanwhile, the Tsar did not view the new Convention as limiting him as a protector of Orthodox Christians living in the Holy Places. Western nations also took their responsibilities to protect the rights of the Sultan under the Convention quite seriously.[19] The British view of Tsar Nicholas' intentions was coloured by Lord Aberdeen's understanding that, if the Empire collapsed, no one nation would fill the vacuum left by the Sultan's absence. It was also the Tsar's assumption that Britain would assist Russia in maintaining its interests in the Ottoman Empire. Implicit in this assumption was the belief that no other nation, especially France, would have influence in the Porte.[20] Lulled into complacency by the Tsar's assurances of peace, it became clear why Aberdeen was blind any threat coming from St Petersburg. Certainly no one in the Cabinet wanted war, and Aberdeen, at least, was sympathetic to Nicholas' concern for Christians who lived under the heavy hand of the Turkish Sultan. After all, Aberdeen considered the Tsar an old friend, whereas he looked upon the parvenu ruler of France with suspicion.

Although others in the Cabinet may have had some qualms about identifying themselves with the autocratic Sultan, the clear-sighted Palmerston had no such reservations about Britain's goals in the east. To him, if the Ottoman Empire collapsed, Russia would fill the void and exert its hegemony over the eastern Mediterranean. In turn, this would precipitate a war with France, destroying the peace and upsetting the balance of power. Palmerston did not want war in 1853, nor did he think that the Tsar wanted war, but he knew that the temptation to exploit the Sultan's vulnerability would be too great. Therefore, he was convinced that any hint of Russian designs on the Porte must be met with a clear and firm response. Speaking of the Russians, he told Clarendon, 'If others are firm they will stop or recede; if others recede or falter, they advance and rush in.'[21] However, any effort to put the Tsar on notice ran the risk of being neutralized by Aberdeen's private assurances of Britain's continuing friendship with Russia.

Tensions in the Porte escalated dramatically with the arrival of two formidable men. In February, the Tsar sent the tactless Prince Menshikov as his emissary to the Sultan. His mission was quite plain: to intimidate the Turks into obsequiously accepting the Russian sphere of influence in the empire. By April, a second individual arrived on the scene in the person of the veteran diplomat Stratford Canning, later created Lord Stratford de Redcliffe. Stratford was guardedly hopeful that reform was possible under Britain's guidance. Following Britain's dictates, however, put Stratford in a double bind. Dependency on Britain was preferred to having the Sultan look to France or Russia but, when such reliance was take for granted, the Sultan could be lulled into complacency, thus slowing reform initiatives.[22] Stratford left Constantinople in 1852, but within a year he returned to address the growing crisis provoked by Prince Menshikov.

Ignoring the terms of the 1841 Straits Convention, Menshikov called for a return to the 1774 agreement, giving Russia a protectorate over the Christians of the Ottoman Empire. Stratford, who came to Turkey with no intention of being drawn into a war, found himself acting on his own initiative when an indecisive Cabinet failed to act. The Cabinet dithered throughout June until, on 3 July, Russian troops invaded Moldavia. It finally took an initiative from Austria, who had the most to lose from Russian troop movements in the Balkans, to call a meeting of the Great Powers in July. From this came the Vienna Note, which was sufficiently ambiguous to allow both Russia and Turkey to interpret it in their own way. Russia read it as permitting it to prolong its occupation of Moldavia, whereas the Sultan asked for clarifying amendments. Supported now by impatiently bellicose populations, the Turks and the Russians could ill afford to compromise their positions. By 23 September, Aberdeen and Clarendon, concerned that the Sultan faced imminent danger, ordered that the British join the French fleet in passing through the Dardanelles. Aberdeen's greater fear was that something had to be done to appease the public's growing Russophobia and to keep Palmerston and Russells from resigning. At a Cabinet meeting on 7 October, Palmerston demanded that any Russian ship entering the Black Sea be seized and taken to Turkish ports. The Cabinet would not agree, but they did allow for British action if the Russians crossed the Danube or attacked the Turkish coast.

By 11 October, despite Stratford's renewed efforts at peace, the Turks declared war on Russia, perhaps in an attempt to draw the British in with them. They may have calculated correctly, for news of the Turkish declaration against Russia was greeted with clamorous enthusiasm from all sectors of the British population. Predictably, the radical patriot Roebuck called for action against the autocratic tsar, but others also caught the war fever, including Karl Marx who found a common enemy in Tsar Nicholas,[23] while Cobden and Bright and their pacifist followers virtually stood alone and were hated by the British public for it.

Palmerston's differences with Aberdeen over the crisis in the Porte gave him an opportunity to outline his views on war in general and the use of deterrence in particular. Writing to Aberdeen on 1 November 1853, he said,

> Peace is an Excellent Thing, & war a great misfortune, But there are many Things More valuable than peace, and many Things Much worse than war. The maintenance of the Ottoman Empire belongs to the First Class. The occupation of Turkey by Russia belongs to the Second. But we passed the Rubicon when we first took Part with Turkey and sent our Squadrons to Support her, and when England and France have once taken a Third Power by the Hand, that Third Power *Must* be carried in safety through the Difficulties in Which they may be involved.[24]

At the same time as the government was facing the crisis over the Eastern Question, Lord John Russell tried to revive parliamentary reform. His name had been identified with 'Finality' and with opposition to any extension of reform beyond the 1832 Act. However, as he searched for an issue that would propel him into the Prime Minister's office, Russell became the chief advocate of a new reform bill. His version would have disenfranchised more constituencies and would have extended the suffrage to more of the middle class. Unlike the Whigs' seizure of the initiative in 1832, his timing was less than propitious. By mid-century, the public was ready to reflect on its many accomplishments. The British people could feel smugly, self-satisfied that they did not have to undergo the destructive revolutions of 1848 to become an advanced civilization, so epitomized by the Crystal Palace Exhibition of 1851. Russell's ambitious reach for higher office had exceeded his grasp of the temper of the time, and he seemed equally insensitive to the anti-reform attitude within his own party and among the ministerial leaders. Aberdeen and Graham were sympathetic to the bill being advanced in Parliament, but Palmerston strenuously objected, asserting that Russell's measure would open the way to democratizing amendments, enfranchising the working class. Saying that he would not be 'dragged through the dust by John Russell', Palmerston became the symbol of anti-reformism and a major block to any significant change in Britain until his death in 1865.[25]

His opposition to Russell's bill was as much about politics as it was about principle. Ever since Russell had dislodged him from the cabinet in December 1851, and then Palmerston had had his 'tit-for-tat' revenge in January 1852, it was clear that the two men's careers were on a collision course. During the negotiations that led to the Aberdeen coalition, Palmerston was prepared to join Russell in a new ministry but would not serve under him. For Russell's part, he fixed his gaze on being prime minister. Russell's fixation on 10 Downing Street was equalled only by Palmerston's opposition to it. Therefore, his opposition to Russell's reform bill was as much a campaign against Lord John's ambitions to reshape a new Cabinet. So strong was Palmerston's desire to stop Russell and reform that, on 10 December 1853, he used the ultimate weapon of his resignation, knowing full well that Aberdeen could not afford to accept it.[26] Palmerston felt that the coalition needed him if they were to survive, more than he needed them. Certainly, the events of the next few weeks seemed to confirm this, as the political drama left the controlled setting of Cabinet rooms and was played out in the public arena.

On 11 December, news reached the government that the Turkish fleet had been utterly destroyed by the Russian navy at Sinope, with the loss of all their ships and 4000 men. Even the impetuous Stratford had warned the Turks in November that it would be too dangerous to take on the Russians alone.[27] These details did not bother the British press who trumpeted the news of the 'massacre of Sinope' to a reading public feverishly caught up in growing war hysteria. The press quickly assigned blame to Aberdeen for ignoring Palmerston's call for action, and went on to attribute Palmerston's resignation to the Sinope disaster.[28] Palmerston coyly admitted that it was his opposition to Russell's reform bill that triggered his resignation but said nothing about his foreign policy differences with Aberdeen, leaving the newspapers, especially the *Morning Post*, to fan the flames of public agitation. At this point, the public's perception of what had happened had taken on a life of its own, beyond the control of the ministry. In this highly charged environment, Palmerston rode a crest of popularity while Aberdeen was pilloried for his hesitancy to confront the Russians. In the glare of this publicity, it mattered little that the government had protested to the Russians over their brutality or that the British fleet had joined the French navy to take the offensive at Sebastapol. Nor did it quiet the public when Palmerston accepted overtures to rejoin the Cabinet now that he was satisfied that the movement for parliamentary reform would be posponed.[29]

In all that had passed in less than a week, Palmerston had shown that he was the master of events. On the face of it, by using his resignation as a weapon to foil attempts at parliamentary reform, he demonstrated that he was politically indispensable. When coalition members agreed to defer parliamentary reform for further study, the momentum was lost and in April a tearful Russell reluctantly withdrew his bill. His retreat meant facing the fact that the nation was seeking leadership elsewhere. In opposing reform, Palmerston provided the public with a new banner to march under. The feverish support for Britannia's flag, especially when waved in defence of liberal causes abroad, turned the public's attention away from domestic issues to international affairs. By 1853, Palmerston's support in the country had shifted to a broad middle-class audience who, already possessing the vote, had lost their enthusiasm for more extensive suffrage. Meanwhile, the radicals, intoxicated by the growing enthusiam to put things right in the Near East, were now willing to forgive Palmerston's reform lapses so long as he was willing to fight for it abroad. Instead, they found an another target for their criticism at Court in the person of Prince Albert. With the Queen beyond the pale of respectable criticism, Albert became a surrogate object of ridicule for the press's editorial jibes. To the *Morning Post* and the *Globe* he personified the Russophilic forces bent on driving Palmerston from office. Clearly Palmerston and his allies in the press had turned the tables on Aberdeen and the Court. His resignation was not a victory for his critics but, instead, it was a calculated gamble to test his popularity and his political indispensability.

His defeat of Russell was quickly followed by a second victory. On 27 February, the coalition finally sent its ultimatum to Russia to withdraw its troops from the Danubian principalities of Wallachia and Moldavia. After an inordinate delay, a joint declaration of war was issued from London and Paris on 28 March, and a Western alliance between France and Britain was announced on 10 April. Austria and Prussia chose to go their own way by forming a bi-partite alliance on 20 April in which they swore not to make a compact with any other state. Clearly, the two central powers wished to stay aloof from France and Britain as they gingerly approached a possible confrontation with Russia. If Austria and Prussia had allied with the Western Powers, the assumption was that the Tsar, faced with such a multilateral force, would have given way readily. Still, even when Austria did act alone, the Tsar withdrew his troops from Moldavia and Wallachia. What followed changed the course of the Crimean War and the fate of Austria. The Russian evacuation from the Danubian region moved Britain and France to shift the theatre of battle. A confrontation in Poland would require the unlikely cooperation of Prussia, and entry through the Baltic meant having Sweden's acquiescence. Only the Black Sea region remained a possibility, which made sense to those who saw that Britain and France had an obvious naval advantage over the Russians. Moreover, once Austria rid herself of the Russian danger in the Danubian provinces, she retreated into a passive mode. In keeping a sizeable army on the borders of Galicia, the Tsar may have still perceived a danger from Austria, but the reality was that the war's centre of gravity had turned eastward.

Aberdeen's policy of avoidance was offset by Palmerston's forthright commitment to engage the Russians in the Crimea. By mid-June, he had provided his colleagues with a detailed plan of attack. Rather than becoming bogged down in Wallachia or Moldavia, he wanted to strike directly at the Black Sea naval base of Sebastopol, with a combined force of 25,000 British and 30,000 French troops. Most of the Cabinet agreed with Palmerston and where/there was some uncertainty about details, they left this to the commanders in the field. Only the Secretary of State for War, the Duke of Newcastle, speculated on Britain's unreadiness and even hinted at disastrous consequences. Even Aberdeen fell in line with the Cabinet's final decision of 29 June to proceed.[30]

From all indications, this was Palmerston's war. Curiously, however, as the conflict progressed, his name became more and more disassociated from it. Almost from the outset, the war effort was marked by poor judgement, incompetence and factors beyond the control of the commanders. Yet none of the blame for this found its way back to Palmerston. Lord Raglan, the British commander and veteran of the Napoleonic wars, believed optimistically that Sebastopol could be taken quickly, but the campaign constantly ran into difficulties. The allied forces did not arrive in the Crimea until 24 September, and even when the joint forces defeated the Russians, as at the Alma on 20 September, they were slow to pursue the enemy. The Russians, scuttling their fleet in the harbour, obstructed the naval attack on Sebastopol. Later victories at Inkerman and Balaklava were marred by the news of enormous casualties, numbering 6000 dead, with some 8000 wounded or sick from cholera. The mood of the British public, which had been so enthusiastic in its support of the war effort, dramatically turned as grim reports arrived from war correspondents such as William Howard Russell. Nothing that the generals or politicians could say could soften these newspaper accounts, reported for the first time from the war front.

It was bad enough to hear of the war toll rising due to the miscalculations of generals who were past their prime, but the public outrage soared on learning that men died unnecessarily in field hospitals because of careless procedures and shockingly unsanitary conditions. A family friend of Palmerston, Florence Nightingale, attempted to redress these problems with her call for reforms, but not before the death toll mounted. An unforeseen cold winter added to the suffering of the troops, who had thought that the campaign would end before Christmas. A stunned public began to turn their attack upon the Aberdeen government once again. They had done so months earlier in their bellicosity towards Russia; now they did so in their revulsion at what the war had produced. Members of the Cabinet were aware of the incompetence in the Crimea, but were slow to take action. Lord Raglan's conduct was criticized yet there seemed to be no one of his stature to replace him.[31] At home, the focus turned on the Duke of Newcastle, the Secretary of State for War and the Colonies, who had been agonizingly slow to undertake medical reforms in the field hospitals. By mid-November, with the public clamouring for change, Russell stepped forward to propose that the office of Secretary at War be abolished, an indirect strike at Newcastle and his leader Aberdeen.[32] The Peelite members of the Cabinet saw this as a veiled attack upon Aberdeen and one more attempt by Russell to advance himself as Prime minister. His continuing presence in the Cabinet was valued only because his absence might bring on its collapse. In continuing along his self-destructive path, Russell resigned in protest over the Cabinet's refusal to take his advice. On 25 January 1855, J. A. Roebuck, once the enthusiastic supporter of the conflict, turned critic, and moved for a parliamentary inquiry into the government's conduct of the war. It was for all intents and purposes a motion of censure against the government that carried by a margin of 305 to 157 votes.[33]

As the queen searched for a replacement for Aberdeen, it was clear that Palmerston would be at the centre of any new Cabinet arrangement. Consequently, when she asked Lord Derby as leader of the Tory Opposition to form a new government, he knew that he would have to include Palmerston in it.[34] Palmerston could not easily refuse to join the Derby government although various obstacles did stand in the way. Palmerston would not join without Clarendon returning to the Foreign Office, but Clarendon detested Derby. Various political combinations were considered but none seemed workable. Palmerston seemed to be the inevitable choice as Prime Minister, and after further negotiations with some Peelite allies, a new ministry, with Palmerston as prime minister, was formed on 5 February 1855.[35] In certain respects, the Aberdeen coalition was reborn consisting of Gladstone at the Exchequer, Clarendon back in the Foreign Office, Herbert in charge of the Colonial Office and Sir James Graham at the Admiralty. Even Russell was brought on board but only to be sent to the newly initiated peace talks in Vienna where he could be kept conveniently away from British domestic politics.

Despite the seeming inevitability of the new Palmerston regime, it was not entirely without problems. When Palmerston accepted Roebuck's motion for an inquiry into the conduct of the war, the Peelites in the Cabinet objected to what they called an unconstitutional intrusion of the executive and quit the government on 21 February. Palmerston quickly filled their places with Whigs and the government endured. Russell, still embittered by his lack of advancement, resigned in July and went off to sow dissension among the Whigs. Apart all from these defections, there were rumours of Palmerston's failing health, advancing age, and lack of energy to perform his tasks as prime minister.[36] Meanwhile, an unfriendly queen, the Manchester Liberals, and the unified (but outnumbered) Tories remained constant thorns in his side. Notwithstanding his critics, Palmerston succeeded because so many others around him failed. Aberdeen's name had become fatally identified with British failures in the Crimea. Russell's attempts at advancing his own cause had alienated fellow Whigs, and the Peelites' reputation temporarily suffered for their recent abandonment of Palmerston. Meanwhile, the Derbyites languished on the sidelines, practising a passive policy of watchful waiting. Palmertston was left holding centre stage, still the people's favourite.

Palmerston's continuing popularity in 1855 was sustained by the hope that only he could execute those military reforms that would produce a military victory and an honourable peace. As the numbers of casualties continued to rise in the summer months, Palmerston pressed for medical reforms. He was slower, however, to address the incompetence that plagued the command structure, so rooted in aristocratic privilege.[37] Palmerston's vulnerability on this issue became manifestly obvious when Henry Layard, an avowed supporter of the Crimean War, became the outspoken champion of reforms abolishing the aristocracy's monopoly of the army. His election as a radical MP then gave him a platform from which he zealously pressed his demands. Palmerston cleverly attempted to keep Layard out of opposition by inviting him into the government but to no avail. Using both Parliament and the public platform, Layard kept up his attacks upon the aristocracy, while demanding that equal opportunities be given to the common man. In an attempt to avoid a direct confrontation, Palmerston argued that Layard's own military rise from his middle-class origins demonstrated that there was no impediment to advancement. However, this did not stop the House from considering a motion of censure against the government for upholding aristocratic privilege in the army. Only Palmerston's acceptance of an amendment to remit the question to a committee of inquiry avoided a ministerial defeat.[38] Although Palmerston admitted abuses in the system, he would not allow the officer corps to be democratized, just as he was unyielding in his opposition to the expansion of parliamentary reform.

Meanwhile, as the summer approached, the reports from the Crimea suggested that the war was winding down. Although an attack on the Redan fortress in Sebastopol had failed, a later French assault on the Malakova fortress in September forced the Russians at last to surrender Sebastopol. Other British setbacks followed, but by late November Palmerston realized that an end was near for Russia.[39] By the end of November, the Russian Black Sea fleet had been destroyed and, as 1856 approached, an allied attack upon St Petersburg was threatened. France and Austria welcomed the prospect of peace, but, for Palmerston, greater challenges lay ahead. After the conquest of

Sebastopol, he told his brother William, 'our danger will then begin – a danger of peace, not a danger of war.'[40] Palmerston knew that the British people's bellicosity had remained feverishly high and would not be satisfied by a compromise peace. 'I can fancy how I should be hooted in the House,' he told Clarendon, 'if I were to say we had agreed to an imperfect arrangement about one of the most important points.' The important point in question was Austria's proposal that the Black Sea merely be neutralized and not entirely rid of Russia's naval presence. Palmerston had made it quite clear that Great Britain had gone to war in the Crimea not so much to protect the Sultan as to prevent the Russians from gaining territory from Turkey.[41]

From Palmerston's standpoint, the central issue for negotiation in 1856 was the status of the Russian fleet in the Black Sea. Russia's representative, Gorchakov, working in tandem with the Austrian Foreign Minister, Count Buol, responded by proposing the free navigation of the Black Sea. However, this was out of the question for Palmerston.[42]

Once it was clear that Palmerston would brook no compromise with the Russians, both Austria and France stiffened their demands with an ultimatum to Tsar Alexander that Vienna would soon join the war on the allied side. Now facing diplomatic isolation by all the Great Powers except Prussia, Russia accepted Austria's terms. However, the question still to be answered at the Peace Congress scheduled to meet in Paris in late February 1856 was whether or not these terms would be acceptable to Palmerston and the British people, who were left without a decisive victory to show that they had won the war. Clarendon, Britain's chief representative at the Congress, knew that Napoleon leaned towards peace and, therefore, if Britain had to return to the battlefield, it would do so without France.[43]

The alternative for Clarendon was either to soften Palmerston's demands or to confine his threats to the peace table. At the same time, he had to act as Palmerston's mouthpiece in out-manoeuvring those delegates who pressed for their own agenda. Clarendon, for example, sought to consult Napoleon directly in an attempt to outflank the manoeuvrs of France's pro-Russian Foreign Minister, Count Walewski. The British were also suspicious of attempts by Count Orlov, the Russian representative, to divert the delegates from the original terms of the armistice. For example, Palmerston rejected outright his proposal that the demilitarization of the Black Sea had to be matched by Britain's demilitarization of their fortifications on Heligoland. Of Orlov, Palmerston said, 'He will stand out for every point for which he thinks he has a chance of carrying, and he has all of the cunning of a half-civilized savage.'[44] In addition, Napoleon III had to be dealt with carefully, making sure that he did not use the Congress for his own lofty and self-aggrandizing purposes. As Palmerston tried to stiffen the French spine against Russian intrigues, the Emperor's price for such a commitment escalated. His private conversations with Clarendon shifted from making specific territorial and military demands upon Russia to talk of broad schemes for the dissolution of old empires and the creation of fledgling nations. Exhibiting a visionary approach to the future that made Palmerston nervous, the emperor was prepared to take Europe on a new course, abandoning the Concert of the Powers system (created after the Congress of Vienna in 1815) in order to remake the map of Europe.[45] Palmerston, however, had fought the Crimean war to contain Russia's ambitions in the Near East, not to open the door to revolutionary change.

The immediate business before the Congress gathered in Paris on 25 February 1856 was to produce peace terms that provided protection for Turkish sovereignty, defined the limits to naval power in the Black Sea, and determined the status of the Danubian principalities. Palmerston was in no position to impose draconian terms upon Russia since Britain could not return to the battlefield alone. Throughout the war, British troop strength had been low, and by 1856 their force was less than twenty per cent of the total Allied force in the Crimea.[46] The question remained whether the British people, despite their unflagging bellicosity, would continue to support a war if it had to shoulder the burden alone. Some compromise, therefore, was required, which meant giving way on some terms in order to stand firmly on others. After much wrangling between Clarendon and Orlov, the Russians agreed to demilitarize the Black Sea. The Russians also withdrew their warships from the Black Sea while maintaining their presence in the Sea of Azov. These Black Sea concessions alone represented a British victory as they had achieved the main object of the war. The other provisions of the Treaty of Paris, however, provided cold comfort for the British. Russia had to surrender Bessarabia but they ceded only some territory at the mouth of the Danube. Palmerston was disappointed that the Russians retained control over Circassia and the Crimea and that the Danubian principalities, Moldavia and Wallachia, were combined into the new state of Romania. It did not please Palmerston that Turkey had only nominal authority over Romania because it became the locus of ardent Christian nationalism which threatened the

Turks' Muslim hegemony. More grievous to the British was the inclusion of provisions that were only marginally related to the peace. According to the Declaration of Paris, the right of naval seizure, something that the British had fought for in the war of 1812, was now to be denied under international law. For the proud British public, still yearning for a conclusive victory over the Russians, this was the last straw. After the treaty was signed on 30 March 1856, Palmerston put the best face on it but its proclamation was met by hisses in the City. The Queen was also unhappy that her army had not ended the war with a resounding victory, but Palmerston mollified her by reasoning that the resumption of hostilities was impossible.

The Crimean War had been the greatest challenge to Britain's status as a Great Power since 1815 and was a test of her institutional strength since the passage of the 1832 Reform Act.[47] It appears that she did not pass that test very well, at least as judged by the same public that had encouraged the war effort. Provoked by questions posed in the *Times*' editorials, the people wondered how such a gifted nation could have failed to achieve a glorious victory. In addition to the military commanders, few were spared from criticism. Certainly, the Aberdeen coalition could not avoid being attacked. Aberdeen, it was manifestly clear, was not a war leader, was blind to Russia's threats to Turkey and was indecisive when action was called for. Newcastle, too, could not grasp the magnitude of the crisis in the Crimea and lacked the energy to take the initiative in rebuilding the army. War and army reform were not Gladstone's strong suit, and, by the time Roebuck's motion had shaken the government, it was too late for him and his allies to help the government.[48]

Even in victory it could hardly be said that Britain won a triumphant war or a satisfactory peace. A total of 22,737 lives were lost in gaining what Russia had earlier conceded under the Four Points of 1854. As noted, Palmerston was satisfied that at least Russia was no longer a threat to the Turks in the Black Sea, but the treaty was no guarantee that the Eastern Question had been settled. Russia had left the Black Sea reluctantly and would return once the Great Powers became distracted by events in Germany. Moreover, the desire to protect the integrity of the Turkish Empire by overseeing the establishment of a progressively liberal system of government turned out to be a unrealizable dream. Compared to Britain, France emerged as the greater winner, with Napoleon III seizing centre stage at the Paris Peace Congress in an attempt to revise the 1815 settlement.

Some historians share the view that the Crimean War was a major test of Britain's standing in the world and a challenge to Palmerstonian foreign policy. Although troubled by Great Power interventionism, civil wars and revolution, Europe had avoided the onset of a continental war since 1815. More to the point, no one since Napoleon had challenged Britain's vaunted naval superiority, her economic primacy, or her role as the champion of constitutionalism and liberalism until the battle was joined with Russia in 1854. It might also be argued that no one had more forcefully shaped the contours of the struggle in the Crimea – thereby enhancing Britain's reputation as the savior of the civilized world – than Palmerston. Ironically, he enjoyed the people's applause for championing a war that was to prove unsatisfactory and a peace that was to be widely criticized. From the outset of the Crimean crisis, he had shielded himself from criticism. As Home Secretary he took no responsibility for the indecision and drift into war, while at the same time acting as the public's cheerleader in favour of hostilities. When the war began in earnest and Britain's fortunes turned sour, criticism for incompetence in the field and in high places fell on others. Indeed, as men like Russell and Aberdeen fell by the wayside, Palmerston became the indispensable man of the hour. When threatened by serious criticism, such as Layard's attack upon the aristocratic establishment, Palmerston wisely made calculated retreats without admitting defeat. Even when news of the Paris Peace Treaty was booed, Palmerston was cheered for bringing an unhappy war to an end and for putting the Russian bear in its place. The Cabinet fell in line, a vote of confidence was won to the cheers of the public, and a friendlier Queen Victoria awarded Palmerston the Order of the Garter in April 1856.[49]

Despite the public's support, Palmerston's government was persistently under siege by his former allies, unhappy that their ambitions were never realized. The new parliamentary session of February 1857 offered an occasion for such an attack when Gladstone, whose ambitions for office grew in proportion to his absence from it, tried to attract supporters. He attacked the ministers' budget but it rebounded on him when his motion lost 286 votes to 206.[50] He had underestimated the stolid but smart Chancellor of the Exchequer, George Cornewall Lewis, and his skill in providing a budget, which lowered income tax and gradually reduced sugar and tea duties as well. Nor did it help Gladstone's cause that his hard-edged tone alienated as many MP's as it attracted. Clearly, there was an opportunity here for Gladstone to coalesce with his former Tory friends among the Tories. However, was such a reunion worth the risk of awakening Peelite–Conservative hatred? Meanwhile, as Gladstone tentatively coquetted with the Derbyites, he drifted away from his Peelite allies, thereby risking the prospect of falling between the cracks and into political isolation.

Russell, too, tried to undermine his former ministerial allies by waving the banner of reform, again hoping that some would rally around it. On 19 February 1857, he spoke in favour of a £10 suffrage requirement in both the counties and the boroughs, which attracted votes from liberals normally supportive of Palmerston. The motion failed when Palmerston's die-hards joined frightened conservatives, but clearly the issue of parliamentary reform could not be ignored. Groups such as the Liberation Society and other advanced liberals were tempted to trade their loyalty to Palmerston for electoral changes. Palmerston, sensitive to this erosion of support, complained that the reform-minded Ryder Street Committee were 'trying to pack the parliament with ballot men willing and unwilling'.[51] The reform movement, although hardly a juggernaut, threatened Palmerston's base of support.

Still, apart from his erstwhile friends, the official Opposition offered little threat to Palmerston's political ascendancy. The Derbyites, wrongly relying on Palmerston's former friends being his worst enemies, continued to follow a strategy of watchful waiting. They commanded a united following but, lacking the numbers to sustain a working majority, they were not a ministerial alternative. Derby was too inflexible for middle-of-the-road voters, and Disraeli had not fully won the trust of members of his own party.[52] Others who numbered among the predictable anti-Palmerston forces were a broad array of radicals, such as Cobden and Bright and their Manchester School followers, whose peace policies still ran against the grain of a patriotic nation.

Rather than risk attacks where he was most vulnerable (namely domestic reform), foreign affairs remained in the forefront of Palmerston's national policy. For more than a decade, he had cultivated the British national appetite for constitutionalism abroad, antipathy for autocratic regimes and pride in their perception of themselves as a civilizing force in the world. By focusing on such an agenda, he distracted the public and their radical leaders from domestic grievances while satisfying their desire to uphold moral causes abroad. It has been suggested that, before Palmerston occupied the political limelight in mid-century, Whigs, Liberals and radicals defined national policy in terms of reform programmes that caught the public's attention. When the steam went out of reform as a driving issue in the mid-Victorian era, Palmerston filled the void with a parade of foreign policy precepts for the public to march behind. He could not win the people's favour by propagating parliamentary reforms, first because he opposed them and, secondly, because others had pre-empted the field. Palmerston's only recourse was to play his strong suit: to make foreign policy the chief national interest and to ensure that his name was identified with British successes abroad.

The Crimean victory had buoyed up Palmerston's popularity but other foreign entanglements raised questions about his mastery of events. While Palmerston's forward policy had won him the cheers of the British people, it left behind in several countries a residue of ill feeling that did not heal with time. In China, despite the terms of the Treaty of Nanking of 1842, which aimed at settling merchants' claims, tensions persisted between the two nations. Under the treaty, Shanghai, Canton and other cities were declared 'treaty ports', open to foreign trade. Significantly, Hong Kong was also ceded to Britain, and merchants' claims for the sale of opium were paid. Meanwhile embittered Chinese officials, engulfed in their deepening xenophobia for the west, chafed at granting such privileges. Anglo-Chinese relations were further complicated by the fact that the Treaty of Nanking did little to stem the traffic in opium despite the Chinese government's objections. Palmerston's overall attitude towards opium was that the Chinese could no more ban opium smoking than they could effectively prohibit alcohol consumption. As a practical matter, it would be far better, he thought, to legalize and tax the trade in it.[53] In the end, unlike his persistent enforcement of the ban on the slave trade, it was the doctrine of free trade and not the humanitarian argument that prevailed.

After 1842, Anglo-Chinese relations were further aggravated by incidents involving minor conflicts between British subjects and native Chinese people. Often the local governor, acting on his own initiative and with little chance of waiting for guidance from London, made the situation much worse by dealing with the Chinese harshly. Conflict escalated after 1855, after Palmerston returned to office as prime minister. The new Governor of Hong Kong used the seizure of the *Arrow*, a pirate ship flying British colours, as the basis for shelling the city of Canton. Looting, arson and general mayhem followed, leading to a state of war.

Shaken by news from Canton, the Cabinet voted to send forces to the area but found that Members of Parliament disagreed with Palmerston's new forward policy in Asia. Taking the moral high ground, Richard Cobden was able to cobble together an unusual coalition of nonconformist radicals, Russellite Whigs, Derbyites and Peelites to move a censure motion against the government. Palmerston's response characterized the Chinese as barbaric people who had summarily beheaded British citizens and their own people. Playing the patriotic card, he characterized his critics as anti-English, as if to remind them of the Don Pacifico affair when the rights of Englishmen had had to be protected. This defence was not enough to save him as the censure motion was passed, 263 votes to 247. Not satisfied with this result, he was ready to put the electorate against the House by asking the Queen for a dissolution.[54]

Confident that he could parlay his intervention in China on top of the wave of popularity still riding high after the Crimean War, Palmerston followed a simple theme in the election. Central to his campaign was the message. 'An insolent barbarian wielding authority at Canton had violated the British flag.'[55] When those words were communicated throughout the kingdom it was clear that Palmerston dared to reach beyond his Tiverton constituents to the nation in appealing to the people's patriotic instincts. His opponents were defenceless, for any criticism of his China policy left them open to questions about their patriotism. Meanwhile, Palmerston did not hesitate to pander to any group which supported his forceful China policy. Middle-class businessmen and other urban interests flocked to Palmerston's side, as did anyone who saw profits coming from the Asian trade. The result was a triumph for Palmerston, winning a margin of 85 seats in the House of Commons, while such outspoken opponents as Cobden, Bright and Layard were defeated. Russell, too, barely recaptured his seat. There was no need for Palmerston to address pressing issues like parliamentary reform when he himself was the issue before the voters. As Lord Shaftesbury noted, 'There seems to be no measure, no principle, no cry, to influence men's minds and determine elections; it is simply, "Were you, or were you not? Are you, or are you not, for Palmerston?"'[56]

Although Palmerston's election victory seemed to have validated his aggressive Chinese policy, there was trouble ahead. In early May 1857, sepoy troops in the East India Company's Bengal Army, refused to use cartridges whose ends had been greased with cow or pig fat. Since using beef fat was as much a sin for Hindus as eating pork would be for Muslims, both groups were offended. This act of defiance mushroomed into a full-scale mutiny, leading to the massacre of British officers and their families. The violence was, in fact, the culmination of grievances which had been mounting for years between the sepoys, Hindu princes and British imperial administrators. News of the mutiny reached Britain in early June, and rumours of savage acts committed against British civilians, including women and children, then created an outcry for action. Surprisingly, as cities like Delhi and Kanpur fell into the hands of the insurrectionists, Palmerston reacted almost nonchalantly, saying that the news was 'distressing by reason of the individual sufferings and deaths, but... not really alarming.... It may lead to establishing our power upon... a firm basis.'[57] Even before reinforcements arrived, British officers in India took it upon themselves to reconquer key cities and wreak their vengeance upon the sepoy rebels. Indian civilians were arbitrarily tortured or killed by the British army as they went about their business. The cry for revenge was also raised in Britain where the public was inflamed by a jingoistic press reporting the ravages of British women and children.

The Sepoy Mutiny of 1857 was arguably a turning-point in Britain's modern imperial history. Clearly, the revolt itself, the recapturing of Delhi and other cities, and the ferocity of the massacres awakened the British to deep, underlying fissures separating the west from the imperial world. By the 1858 India Act, which abolished the East India Company, Palmerston recognized that the 1857 uprising was not an isolated event. Rather, the revolt was a sign of national upheaval, potentially with profound implications. Casting aspersions on the East India Company for the Sepoy Mutiny was ill placed, for its powers had already been eclipsed by the Board of Control and a revamped civil service open to a small but increasing number of native Indians. Nevertheless, the reforms envisioned testified to Britain's fundamentally defensive posture towards India in the future. Henceforth, India, it was generally recognized, would be 'held by the sword', as Sir William Denison, the new Governor of Madras, put it.[58] This meant that, as a precautionary act against future mutinies, the natives' participation in the army would be lessened, its artillery diminished and the number of British troops increased. In general, the ministry tried to ply a course between turning the British military presence into an army of occupation and undermining the morale of the native troops. It was, they agreed, an intractable problem, which did not lend itself to easy solutions.

Leaving aside the more profound implications for the Empire, the suppression of the Sepoy Mutiny and the passage of the India Act kept the parliamentary Opposition at bay in 1857. Palmerston was also able to neutralize Russell's effort at moving a major parliamentary reform bill with his own limited measure. Then, ironically, the very issue that helped him to curry the public's favour was used against him in 1858. In January, a republican follower of Mazzini, Felici Orsini, attempted to assassinate Napoleon III and his wife. Even in failing, Orsini succeeded in implicating Italian refugees who used London as a base. Eager to maintain cordial ties with Napoleon while discouraging the use of Britain as a base for terrorist operations, Palmerston tried to soften the French public's indignation by moving the Conspiracy to Murder Bill. In doing so, however, he pleased the French but enraged his erstwhile followers at home. It was seen to be an act of betrayal for this personification of John Bull to have so readily surrendered to the French. The disparate opposition groups in Parliament seized the moment by falling behind the radical Thomas Milner Gibson, who put forward a motion criticizing the government's conciliatory policy. Feeling ill-used by the radicals, Palmerston reacted angrily against them but, in doing so, he unwittingly united all of the opposition against him. The Tories, at first inclined to support the Conspiracy to Murder Bill, now joined Russell, Roebuck and the Peelites in carrying Gibson's motion, 234 votes to 215.[59] It is possible that if it hadn't been the Orsini crisis which spelt defeat, then other issues (the India Bill or parliamentary reform) may have done so. Most telling was the realization that the same popular feeling in the country which had contributed to Palmerston's ascendancy also caused his fall from grace. Still, it did not seem likely that the fragile alliance which defeated Palmerston in 1858 would pose a threat to him in the future. More likely was that his successors, Lord Derby's Tory minority government, would act as caretakers until a new political alignment could be formed.

It might be argued that from 1851 to 1858 Palmerstonianism reached its high-water mark. Although it began and ended inauspiciously, with Palmerston's ejection from office in December 1851 and a government defeat in 1858, in the interim years he dominated the political landscape both at home and abroad. It would be disingenuous to say that he merely filled a void due to a lack of better men and measures. He proved to be a man of action who, first as Home Secretary and then as Prime Minister, set the pace in advancing a new style of governmental reform. Having gained a reputation for hard work at the War Office in his early years, Palmerston relished being in power even in old age. Although he may have preferred to have returned to the Foreign Office in 1852, he was not merely marking time at the Home Office from 1852 to 1855. Indeed, it has been said of him that, in advancing educational, health and prison reforms, he innovatively set the tone for future Liberal governments. Relying on the expertise of a new breed of men drawn from Peelite and Whig ranks, he placed a higher value on disinterested efficiency, rational planning and practical results. Although Palmerston did not see himself as responding reflexively to the demands of the people, he did try to strike a balance between what good government could efficiently do for its people and the limits that kept it from pursuing utopian dreams. In laying down the basis for modern Liberal reform, he stole the radicals' thunder without surrendering to them, and took the incipient Liberal Party down a path that William Gladstone and others would follow.[60] In controlling the reform agenda, Palmerston also demonstrated that he and not others would dictate the Liberals' future direction. Russell's frustrated attempts at advancing parliamentary reform was proof positive that such initiatives were impossible without Palmerston's assent. Moreover, the fact that Palmerston saw no urgency in extending the franchise suggests that he, not Russell, had a better sense of the temper of the times and the needs of the people.

While Palmerston may have given some direction to the future course of political reforms, his imprint on British foreign policy was unmistakable. In responding to the 1848 continental revolutions, he was portrayed inaccurately as someone who played to the crowd in sponsoring constitutionalism liberalism abroad. In fact, his use of bluster and bluff to satisfy the public's appetite for flag-waving was balanced by the pragmatic quest for stability and peace. Palmerston's crowd-pleasing declarations against despotism in Italy, for example, were matched by his concern that Austria remained a stabilizing force in central Europe. In short, his pursuit of the lofty goal of constitutional liberalism must be seen in the context of satisfying British interests, which included the British navy's primacy, Britain's domination of world trade and the maintenance of the balance of power. Palmerston's deft merger of these goals was most evident during the Crimean War. In seizing the direction of the war effort from the indecisive Aberdeen, Palmerston satisfied the public appetite for justice against the authoritarian Russian Tsar. At the same time, he knew that it was in Britain's best interest to prop up an autocratic Sultan and maintain the Hapsburg's counter-revolutionary regime in Vienna. Even when pressed by an embittered public not to negotiate a peace with Russia in 1856, he realized that Britain could not pursue the war alone. Still, even when not gaining a complete victory, Palmerstonianism prevailed. The outcries against the war's abuses never touched him and, even although he was defeated on the Conspiracy to Murder Bill in 1858, he was still to see future victories.

5

THE LAST YEARS

On the face of it, Palmerston's defeat in 1858 signalled the beginning of the end of his public life. His advanced age alone militated against his return to office. Now in his seventies, suffering from chronic gout and seemingly exhausted by his labours, he was being written off by Members of Parliament as early as 1855. The 1857 parliamentary election had given him a lease on life, but it was unlikely that the forces that coalesced to bring him down in February 1858 would succeed him. Although the new Tory ministry under Lord Derby's leadership still lacked the strength of a majority, in comparison the Opposition was in disarray. Palmerston's leadership of the opposition in the House of Commons appeared merely titular. He headed a shadow cabinet and held party meetings but beyond that he was seen as a spent force, unable to command a following.[1] Russell was still his obvious rival and their clashing ambitions, catalysed by their differences over parliamentary reform, stood in the way of any reconciliation. When opportunities did arise to attack the ministers, poor communication among Opposition leaders and clever deceptions by Disraeli allowed the government to snatch victories from the jaws of defeat. The opposition, for example, roundly attacked the Tories' version of an India Bill in May 1858, but it survived when the opposition leaders' efforts disintegrated into squabbling. This was described well by the radical Trelawny, when he said 'we are merely on the stage on which a fencing match or triangular duel is taking place between the great party leaders opposed to the Ministry'.[2] Well-conceived but badly executed censure motions aimed at the ministers were awkwardly withdrawn by the opposition, fearful that divisions would only reveal the weakness in their ranks.

As the 1858 session proceeded, Lord Derby's sober, moderate government produced a series of modest but important reforms, suggesting that enlightened improvements could be realized without the overseeing assistance of the Whigs.[3] The property qualifications for MPs were abolished, postal services between the United States and Ireland were established, minor concessions were given to Catholics, and peace was maintained abroad.

As Whigs grumbled amongst themselves about the miserable condition of their party, it was not surprising that blame fell on Palmerston's shoulders. Given his long incumbency in office, he was unused to being in Opposition. He was an elderly neophyte trying to navigate his way through the tricky waters of parliamentary manoeuvring. The task of attacking ministers would have been easier if he still could summon the support of public opinion behind him. Moreover, in 1858, unlike the previous year, his apparent Francophile views caused a rift with the public. Nor did it help matters that he and his ally, Lord Clarendon, were invited to visit France as Napoleon III's guests in November 1858. Palmerston saw the trip as consistent with an earlier one by the royal family aimed at strengthening Anglo-French relations. Vilified by the press, which in the past had trumpeted his causes, his chances for future office seemed doomed. Prince Albert wondered at the transformation in the public's attitude, saying, 'The man who was without rhyme or reason stamped...the man of the people...is now considered the head of a clique, the man of intrigue...in fact hated'.[4] Gladstone, feeling very certain of himself, wrote anonymously in the October 1858 *Quarterly Review*, that 'Come what may, Lord Palmerston shall not again be Minister.'[5]

When the 1859 parliamentary session opened, nothing would have exposed the fissures in the opposition's fragile unity more than the revival of the reform issue. Russell's efforts to raise the question had repeatedly driven a wedge between himself and Palmerston and were likely to do so again. Liberal colleagues may also have felt the necessity to offer the country a reform bill, but Palmerston was satisfied that the 1832 Act sufficed. He feared that extending the franchise to the workers would dangerously democratize the nation by shifting power to the ignorant poor.[6] Meanwhile, John Bright, the free-trade radical, stole the initiative from Russell and the Whigs by taking his case for reform to the country in the winter of 1858. Speaking to crowds on railway platforms and to the nation through a travelling press corps, Bright's populist rhetoric was frightening to the moderates, while the plan's redistributist aspect threatened to alienate the Whigs. Russell recoiled at the shrill tone of these speeches but he was still eager to reach out to the working classes. In February 1859, Disraeli presented a bill to the House of Commons which cautiously allowed for a £10 occupancy franchise in both the counties and the boroughs. The net effect of the bill was to displease both Russell and the radicals who sought a franchise for the respectable, artisan members of the working class, while opposing any effort to deprive the 40-shilling freeholders of their votes in the counties. On 1 April 1859, Russell successfully passed an amendment, by 330 votes to 291, which lowered Disraeli's £10 occupancy franchise to £6. While this vote was a setback for the Derby government, it was not necessarily a personal victory for Russell. Palmerston and other moderates could claim that this was not a pledge for advanced reforms and that the amendment differed little from Disraeli's original bill. Moreover, the Tories' decision to call for new elections, rather than resign, deprived their successors of posing as champions of radical reforms.[7]

When Palmerston sought re-election at Tiverton in late April, the issue of parliamentary reform was eclipsed by the crisis between Italian liberals and Austria. Led by their shrewd premier, Camillo di Cavour, the Sardinians provoked Austria to declare war. This smoldering crisis, with roots in the 1848 revolutions, became an international issue when Cavour played upon Napoleon III's territorial ambitions, beguiling him into assisting in Austria's expulsion from Lombardy–Venetia. Once this agreement was revealed, the Derby government was caught off guard. The Derbyites offended the Austrians by combining declarations of neutrality with sympathy for the Italians' liberal goals.[8]

Given the emerging Italian crisis, the coming election permitted Palmerston to air his views. 'I am very Austrian north of the Alps,' he told Granville on 30 January 1859, 'but very anti-Austrian south of the Alps.' South of the Alps, he explained, the Austrians mismanaged their rule, inviting agitation from the liberals. North of the Alps, he saw that an Austria weakened by an Italian war would not only face Hungarian secession but, Russian encroachment on her borders and the dismemberment of her empire. Austria's claims over Lombardy–Venetia were, he believed, indefensible and he felt that Italy's national and liberal goals would not be satisfied peacefully. Like the Tories, he counselled neutrality but one that was friendlier to France and sympathetic to the British public's anti-papal disposition. In short, Palmerston chose neutrality in war but not in diplomacy. Although hesitant about accepting

Napoleon III's territorial designs, Palmerston saw that the British people would support French intervention in Italy if it meant an end to papal and Hapsburg domination.[9] He underscored these views as he campaigned in Tiverton by steering a clear course between defending Austria's role in Europe as a major power and tolerating a short and limited war of Italian liberation. 'Out of evil good may flow,' he said, 'and we shall rejoice at the issue, though we may regret the miseries which may have preceded it.'[10]

All in all, the 1859 elections appeared to have altered the opposition's relationship with the Derby government very little. The Tories held onto their ministry with 306 seats as against a divided opposition of 350 liberals, radicals and Irish MPs.[11] Palmerston easily retained his seat at Tiverton and re-emerged as the leading liberal spokesman, due in large part to his command of foreign policy issues. In this, he seemed to outpace Russell in his defence of the Italian cause. To be sure, Russell equally deplored what appeared to be the ministry's pro-Austrian stance, but his language was less strident than Palmerston's, who typically made good use of the travelling press to advertise his views to the public.

Since the election did not displace the Tories, in May; Whigs, Peelites, radicals and liberals were busy negotiating a strategy that might lead them into office. Russell's minimal conditions required that Whigs and liberals cooperate with Peelites and radicals in forming a government that would advance an extensive parliamentary reform bill. Palmerston, on the other hand, wanted to avoid making any specific pledges, especially for radical changes in the franchise. Given these differences, any united effort to unseat the Tories would require an understanding between the two men. Russell, tired of fighting his battles for reform in opposition, and longing to realize his ambitions as the leader of a liberal ministry, was open to an alliance to turn out the Tories. In a meeting on 20 May, he and Palmerston found that they could agree on some common policies around which they could form a government. However, the sticking point was who was to lead. Palmerston proposed that both men, depending on the Queen's choice, should agree to serve under each other. Russell, his vanity still standing in the way, would not go that far.[12]

Nevertheless, this meeting lay the groundwork for a historic gathering on 6 June of all shades of liberal opinion at Willis's Rooms. Here, at St James Street, where Almack's Club once stood – a place where a much younger Palmerston danced and gossiped into the night with his future wife and Princess Lieven – came some 280 liberal MPs, including Palmerstonian and Russellite Whigs, Cobdenites and an assortment of Peelites, the Irish and radicals.[13] As each leader rose to speak, a consensus emerged in favour of unity and a willingness on the part of both Palmerston and Russell to serve in a new Cabinet led by either man. Even John Bright, considered a renegade, joined the chorus of solidarity behind a new liberal regime. This extraordinary meeting, seen by most historians as the foundation of the modern Liberal Party, brought together a powerful blend of Whig reformist traditions, Peelite moral impulses, demands for economic efficiency, and radical purposefulness – all qualities that would dominate most Victorian ministries for the last thirty years of the nineteenth century.[14]

How can this extraordinary merger of liberal interests be explained? For the first time since the break-up of parties in 1846, the two-party alignment was restored. For the past fifteen years, party unity had been subordinated to intramural personal and policy differences that had impeded the advancement of coherent reforms. Unlike the tight-knit body of Derbyites, who gloried in their unity at the price of being a perpetual minority, the liberals had more reasons to disagree than agree with each other. In recent years, Palmerston had consistently frustrated aspiring leaders like Russell, Cobden, Bright and Gladstone in their quest for office and the advancement of reforms. Just as consistently, these individuals and their cadres of followers broke ranks to form temporary alliances to turn Palmerston out of office. By June 1859, the liberals realized that there was more to be gained from agreement than disagreement. At one end of the political spectrum, the motives for a liberal alliance were clear. Radicals of the Manchester School, like Bright and Cobden, hoped that they would gain more for their cause by having seats in the Cabinet than being isolated on the backbenches. Radicals like Bright and Milner-Gibson preferred to serve under Russell, but begrudgingly supported Palmerston in return for a radical voice in the Cabinet. This may have been more of a result of Bright's flagging strength in the country and his jealous realization that Palmerston had stolen the public's favour from the radicals, than it was a sign of true agreement on the issues.[15] The Peelites had already begun the process of integration with Palmerstonian liberals as measured by the numbers of those who drifted in and out of his ministries since 1855. There had been flirtations with the Derby government, but differences over reform made any reconciliation with the Tories unlikely. Moreover, Gladstone's sympathies for the Italian liberals were strong enough to pull him into the Palmerstonian camp. Not wanting to be the only obstacle to a liberal merger, he fell in line on the condition that he was given the office of Chancellor of the Exchequer. Russell, too, realized that he did not have the following to form his own government. Although some feared that he might threaten a Palmerston ministry from within, at this point Russell seemed willing to cooperate. Implicit in the willingness to subordinate himself to Palmerston was the belief that the old man's days were numbered.[16]

Transcending all of these motives for cooperation was the immediate concern about the Italian revolution. The recent parliamentary campaign had revealed that the Derbyites' ineptness had brought Europe closer to war. Not surprisingly, when the Whigs proposed a motion of censure against the government, it called for a vote for peace and non-interference. The motion was passed by 323 votes to 310, and the Derbyites resigned.[17]

The Willis Rooms agreement produced a consensus behind the new liberal government but it did not end speculation about the choice of its leader. Russell would have given way to Palmerston as premier residing in the House of Lords if he could lead the House of Commons. Palmerston, however, insisted on being Prime Minister with Russell being elevated to the Lords. Avoiding the difficult decision of choosing between Russell and Palmerston, the Queen, to everyone's surprise, turned to the even-tempered Lord Granville. Although Russell had agreed to act under Palmerston, he would not take third place in a new Cabinet led by Granville. When it became clear that Granville had no stomach for the job, Palmerston then became the obvious choice as Prime Minister.

On 12 June, Palmerston fashioned a new ministry that reflected the sentiments of Willis's Rooms agreement. Aristocratic Whiggery was well represented by Russell in the Foreign Office, Cornewall Lewis at the Home Office, Lord Granville as President of the Council, and Charles Wood as Secretary of State for India. The Peelites were satisfied when Gladstone became Chancellor of the Exchequer, Herbert was made Secretary for War, and the Duke of Newcastle was appointed Colonial Secretary. To please the radicals, Palmerston invited Cobden to join the government, but he refused. John Bright had joined Palmerston on the platform at Willis's Rooms but would not do so in government. The radical's recent speeches attacking the aristocratic system were too shrill for the Whig establishment, so no invitation to join the government was offered.[18] Despite Cobden and Bright's absence, radical surrogates were found in the persons of Thomas Milner-Gibson and Charles Villiers, who both went to the Board of Trade. The inclusion of such radicals completed the progressive alliance inaugurated at Willis's Rooms and constituted the core of the fledgling Liberal Party after Palmerston's death.

Initially, it was the Italian crisis that rallied these liberal interests together in Palmerston's Cabinet. Although caution was being preached at Court and by pro-Austrian elements in the Cabinet, the ministry's key players – Palmerston, Russell and Gladstone – were committed to a decided course of action. Palmerston's Tiverton election speech of April 1859 set out a policy that counselled neutrality because he opposed being part of any war in Italy. Still he was not indifferent to claims that Lombardy and Venetia had rights to self-determination, nor to the issue of Austria's surrender of its territorial claims in the area. He reasoned that, in order for a state to shape its own foreign and commercial policies, it must be free from foreign influences. It was, therefore, in Britain's interest, he concluded, to foster a independent state in Northern Italy. He also speculated that Sardinia would be the nucleus for territorial expansion that might include Parma, Modena, Tuscany and even the Papal States. In making these comments, it is clear that Palmerston had enlarged on views first expressed amidst the chaotic days of the 1848 revolutions.[19] Although still protective of Austria's place in Europe, he now viewed the Hapsburg presence in Italy as an impediment to peace. Secondly, in step with the British public's anti-papal mood, he agreed with Russell that a modern liberal state would be a welcome alternative to the outmoded papal domination of central Italy. Finally, he realized that he could not allow Napoleon III to be the sole sponsor of Italian unification.

This became most evident when Napoleon came to terms with the Hapsburgs by the Treaty of Villafranca of 1859. Under this agreement, the Emperor won Lombardy for Sardinia but at the price of Austria retaining Venetia. Echoing the outrage of the British people, Palmerston condemned this settlement, telling the French ambassador that 'England could never associate herself with such a bad arrangement.'[20] It did not help matters when he later learned that Nice and Savoy would be ceded to France. Curiously, this new turn of events gave Palmerston the best of both worlds. Before Villafranca, it appeared that he was defending Austria against Italian interests. Now he could criticize Napoleon without lessening his support for the Italian cause. Victor Emmanuel, the Sardinian king, found himself in the position of being courted by two lovers. Palmerston tried wooing the king with the argument that Britain was a more reliable ally than France. However, would the Cabinet agree to assist Sardinia militarily? Not only were military guarantees out of the question but even diplomatic initiatives were met with demurs from Victoria and cautious members of the Cabinet.[21] Nevertheless, it was assumed that any policy favourable to Sardinia's role entailed a British guarantee of military support. At the very least, this meant Britain sending a squadron to the Adriatic together with some regimental support. Such involvement, from Palmerston's perspective, was meant to be a deterrent, not a provocation for war. All of this was complicated by the growing Francophobia in the country, which Palmerston was clever enough to convey in the icy tone of his communiqués to Paris.

When seen in the larger context of Napoleon III's other schemes, including his designs on the Crimea, Mexico and Suez, Palmerston did not put anything past the French leader, including an attack on England's vulnerable defences. He was able to use this threat of a French attack to present a rearmament programme to Parliament late in 1859. Earlier in the year, a Royal Commission had recommended rebuilding Britain's endangered dockyards and arsenal. Palmerston adopted this plan and, in addition, proposed more shipbuilding, including an experiment with ironclad vessels.

At this point in the debate over increased arms expenditures, a fundamental difference between Palmerston and Gladstone surfaced, auguring future clashes between the two men. At the heart of the dispute was Palmerston's resolute commitment to rearmament in contrast to Gladstone's desire to alleviate the tax burden by curtailing military spending. Central to Gladstone's 1860 budget was the proposal to abolish the duties on paper. The tax proposal was carried in the House of Commons but, with Palmerston's undisguised encouragement, it failed in the Lords.[22] There were murmurs of resignations but nothing materialized until Gladstone renewed his effort to abolish the paper tax in 1861. This time, support for the measure had dwindled and there was talk of Gladstone resigning. In the end, an accommodation was reached when Gladstone accepted a budget deficit which allowed for both the repeal of the paper duties and for money for Palmerston's arms build-up.[23] According to E. D. Steele, the loss of the paper duties was a minor concession for Palmerston so long as monies could be found for rearmament.[24] More importantly, this incident prefigured other future titanic struggles (such as the struggle over parliamentary reform between Palmerston and Gladstone) but for now Palmerston's leadership prevailed. Instead, as Cornwall Lewis noted, Gladstone had to decide 'to choose to staying [sic] in to eat his words... and going out alone'.²⁵

Meanwhile, in Italy the unification movement had reached its second phase in 1859 when Guiseppe Garibaldi and his radical Red Shirts invaded Sicily and overthrew its Bourbon government. With local republicans amassed behind him, Garibaldi then attacked the mainland, forcing Palmerston to make some difficult diplomatic choices. Given the rising enthusiasm for Garibaldi's romantic adventurism in Britain, support for the republican cause would have been popular, but at this point Palmerston's attention turned to France. He suspected that Napoleon III had agreed with Cavour to support Garibaldi in return for the cession of Genoa and the island of Sardinia. Palmerston had spent most of the spring and summer alternately promising to defend the King of Naples against an attack from Garibaldi, or aiding the republican cause to preclude France from developing a sphere of influence in Italy. This preoccupation with a Napoleonic plot suddenly changed when he received overtures to join the French navy in preventing Garibaldi from crossing the Straits of Messina into Naples. Now disabused of his earlier suspicions that Cavour was acting as Napoleon III's go-between, Palmerton considered the offer. Russell then wisely pointed out that stopping Garibaldi would make Britain look like an enemy of Italian popular feeling. However, by allowing France to obstruct Garibaldi's march, Napoleon alone risked losing Sardinia as an ally. The French Emperor knew better and shrewdly chose inaction over intervention, thereby allowing the Garibaldian expedition to proceed. Although the British fleet remained lurking in the background, the further takeover of Naples, the Papal States and other territories followed unopposed and unassisted by Britain.²⁶

On balance, Palmerston was satisfied with the outcome of events in Italy in 1860. The Italian people had begun that process of self-improvement identified with Palmerston's support for constitutionalism. When Russell triumphantly announced on 27 October 1860 that Great Britain recognized Victor Emmanuel's new Italian government, it was really a celebration of Palmerstonian foreign policy.²⁷ It also pleased Britain that the Italian revolution had produced a constitutional monarchy and not a democracy. Consistent with Palmerston's advocacy of constitutional regimes as a moderate alternative to reactionary government or radical experiments, a unified nation had been created under King Victor Emmanuel without Britain's intervention. Moreover, Palmerston was pleased that Garibaldi had recognized Victor Emmanuel as his king rather than exploiting his victories in Sicily and Naples.[28] More importantly, all this had been achieved without Italy becoming a client state of France. Granted that Palmerston had acquiesced in Napoleon III's acquisition of Nice and Savoy, but in return Austria's retreat from Italy and Sardinia's advance towards unification made that sacrifice worth while. In a sense, Palmerston's Italian victory demonstrated that he could keep a vigilant eye on Napoleon III while still maintaining Anglo-French cooperation. Earlier in 1860, he had proposed that the two nations join in a defensive alliance to protect Romagna, Tuscany and Modena against Austrian intervention. This proposal had been entirely consistent with past efforts to control French ambitions through cooperation rather than confrontation. Similarly, it seemed the wiser course to cultivate those areas where Britain could agree with France rather than focus on points of difference. Both nations agreed that Italy should be free from foreign domination by Austria and from the shadow of papal authority.[29]

While Palmerston oversaw the unification of Italy in 1860, the election of Abraham Lincoln as President signalled the break-up of the United States. Palmerston's reaction to the advent of the American Civil War was a mixed one. As an aristocrat unable to appreciate American republicanism, and put off by their upstart claims to greatness, he viewed them with coolness. In certain respects, Palmerston's anti-American attitude reflected the state of Anglo-American affairs in the first half of the nineteenth century. Given Canada's proximity to the United States, Britain had interests to protect, whether they dealt with boundary disputes, conflicts over the slave trade, or trade issues. Many of these disputes were settled after much diplomatic wrangling. In 1842, the Webster–Ashburton Treaty set the boundaries from the coast of Maine to the Rocky Mountains. In 1850, the Clayton–Bulwer Treaty temporarily settled differences over commercial interests in Central America.[30] Some differences still remained and the coming of the American Civil War was not entirely unwelcome news to Palmerston. A divided United States would slow the advance of America's northern industrial juggernaut and create a southern nation more compatible with British interests. Indeed, Palmerston recognized that an independent Confederacy was an attractive market for British manufactured products.[31] These pragmatic considerations did not keep Palmerston from opposing southern slavery, although he was more interested in outlawing the slave trade than the institution of slavery itself. The Manchester liberals Cobden and Bright joined their hated rivals, the Chartists and Socialists, in championing the Northern cause. Palmerston's ministry was split between those who supported the North and others, led by Gladstone and Russell, who favoured the South. The Queen and Prince Albert, always reluctant to side with rebellious causes, and yet sympathetic to the South's traditionalism, were firmly neutral. Despite ministerial differences, Palmerston prevailed in promoting a thinly disguised form of neutrality that recognized the South as belligerents and not a breakaway body of rebels. Gladstone would have gone further by throwing British support behind the South, but Palmerston, always the hardheaded realist, kept his options open. Even the South's success at the Battle of Bull Run in July 1861, did not move him to shift behind the Confederacy.[32]

The test of Britain's neutrality came soon enough in late 1861. Two Confederate representatives, John Slidell and James Mason, were sent to Britain and France to seek diplomatic recognition. Sailing on the British steamer *Trent*, they were stopped by the United States navy, and taken into custody. The British press, especially Palmerston's allies at the *Morning Post* and the *Times*, published sensational headlines of war while American crowds responded by trumpeting their pleasure at their navy's intervention. Palmerston, calling the arrests a 'gross insult', sent 3000 troops to Canada to back up demands for Mason and Slidell's prompt release. Acting every bit the English bulldog, Palmerston said that the American government would have to accede to Britain's demands and be humiliated or that war might come.[33] Palmerston's bellicosity, however, veiled an effort to give Lincoln and Secretary of State William Seward a way out. Britain's ultimatum allowed the Americans to retreat by offering a simple apology. Other factors also lessened the prospect of hostilities. From the outset of the Civil War, Anglo-French solidarity precluded the Americans from having any possibility of help from Paris. Also, the North would not have diverted her forces from the South to fight the British, nor would Northern banking and commercial interests risk jeopardizing their lucrative trade with Britain.

Nevertheless, other Anglo-American tensions tested Palmerston's commitment to neutrality. In 1862, Palmerston belatedly learned that a Confederate ship, the *Alabama*, was being built at the Birkenhead shipyards. If this vessel were meant for combat against Northern shipping, then it would have been a violation of neutrality. However,

Palmerston claimed that since the British government had no knowledge of the ship's construction, there should be no liability for damages suffered when the *Alabama* later bombarded northern shipping. Meanwhile, the Confederacy was pressing Palmerston to join France in mediating the North–South conflict. Gladstone and Russell also favoured mediation but Palmerston put them off, thinking that Britain might be drawn into the war on the South's side.[34] Instead, he preferred to watch General Lee's advances in Virginia before straying from his neutral course. When word came in 1862 that Lee had failed to defeat the Northern army decisively at the Battle of Antietam, followed by news of Lincoln's issuance of the Emancipation Proclamation freeing the slaves, Palmerston began to mend relations with the United States. In the months that followed, Palmerston remained uncharacteristically quiet, and once the North had won the decisive Battle of Gettysburg, his pugnacity softened. As a result of this, attacks upon British shipping by the Americans for violations of the neutrality laws went unanswered and negotiations with the South broke off.

Although the North's blockade of southern cotton destined for English mills might have tempted Palmerston to react with hostility, he stayed the neutral course.[35] His response to a belligerent Russell was 'The only thing to do seems to be to lie on our oars, and to give no pretext to the Washingtonians to quarrel with us, while, on the other hand, we maintain our rights and those of our fellow-countrymen.'[36] In the past, blockades and attacks upon British shipping would have evoked sharp responses from Palmerston. Now, he was happy to win the public's favour at the Americans' expense in the *Trent* affair, but actual intervention was another matter. As early as December 1860, he said, 'Nothing could be more undesirable than for us to interfere in the dispute, if it should break out.' Later, he was even more convinced that, unless the North was militarily devastated, Britain should refrain from recognizing the South.[37] Despite the great temptation to use gunboat diplomacy to end the American blockade, Palmerston demonstrated admirable restraint in keeping the ministry and public at bay. That the *Trent* affair was resolved peaceably and that Palmerston vigorously tried to avoid any repetition of the *Alabama* claims for damages suggests that there was a softer line to his diplomacy.

Although selective intervention had been effective in dealing with the American Civil War, it fared less well as new crises surfaced in Europe. In January 1863, the Russian Tsar Alexander II, in an effort to quiet Polish demands for autonomy, forcibly recruited Poles into the Russian army. Such heavy-handed action evoked a popular and ill-conceived Polish response, which was brutally crushed by the Tsar's army. The scene brought back memories of the 1831 rising, when the Poles had revolted in an attempt to protect their rights gained under the 1815 Treaty. At the time, Palmerston had stoutly defended the Poles but refused to endanger Russian relations by becoming embroiled in war. Just as there had been enthusiastic supporters of the Polish cause in the 1830s, new cries now went up in the House of Commons. The *Times* took up the public's outcry with headlines calling for intervention. Palmerston's response pleased no one. He angered the radicals because his words of protest went no further. He also annoyed the vigilant Victoria who recoiled at language that might stir up central Europe. Trying to chart a middle course, Palmerston's proposal for the suspension of hostilities fell flat. Earlier in February, Napoleon III had taken the initiative by suggesting that the French, Austrians and the British protest against the actions of Otto von Bismarck, Prussia's new Chancellor, who offered assistance to the Tsar in quelling the Polish revolt. Although Palmerston welcomed Napoleon's willingness to take a harder line against Russia, he saw through the French stratagem and rejected the offer.[38]

France, Austria and Britain made a feeble attempt at proposing that the Tsar grant Poland autonomy but their efforts went no further. Austria welcomed Russia's new troubles but preferred to act cautiously, fearing that its own minorities would follow the Polish example. Napoleon, pressured by French Catholics and Republicans, was willing to risk even a confrontation on the Rhine with Prussia, who had recently aligned itself with Russia against the Poles. Palmerston knew that shifting the focus from Russia to Prussia might drag Britain into an unwanted war. This response to the Polish revolt produced two diplomatic setbacks for Palmerston's government. It was bad enough for Britain to be snubbed diplomatically by the Russians' outright refusal to discuss the Polish question, implying that Palmerston had no role to play in Eastern Europe. The effect on Anglo-French relations was worse. Although it was Napoleon III's recklessness that jeopardized Franco-Russian relations, he blamed Britain for preventing a French victory over Russia.[39]

In November 1863, the French Emperor, acting as the new impresario of European affairs, invited the Great Powers to an international conference in Paris to find a substitute for the 1815 Vienna accords. By issuing this invitation, he virtually proclaimed a death sentence on the international system that had guaranteed European security for the past forty-eight years. He also made himself the arbiter of a broad agenda that might even question the sanctity of boundary lines. The impact in European capitals was profound. Stocks and shares plummeted as principal ministers rushed to send their regrets. The British response was carefully crafted and stinging. Palmerston said that 1863 was not 1815, nor was it 1856. In 1815, Europe was in postwar disarray, which required a thorough restoration of lands and titles. In 1856, peace again had to be restored. That was not true in 1863, he said, and he believed such a congress would only attract ambitious powers seeking to fulfil their aspirations.[40] In reaffirming Britain's commitment to the Vienna accords, Palmerston's government effectively ended their on-going, albeit uneasy, alliance with France.

The benefit of the Anglo-French *entente* became most evident once it ended, for it effectively left both nations in diplomatic isolation. As if to underscore Britain's newly discovered vulnerability, the unresolved Danish question came back to haunt Palmerston. He knew that the German states might act at the expense of the Danes over the contested two duchies, Schleswig and Holstein. According to the Treaty of London of 1852, the duchies were to remain inseparable under the Danish heir apparent, Duke Christian of Glucksberg. Faced with a highly complex and intractable situation, this seemed to be the best that the London delegates could do. Later, Palmerston made the waggish comment that only three persons understood the dilemma of the duchies: one was Prince Albert and he was dead, another was a Danish statesman, now consigned to a lunatic asylum, and the third was himself and he had forgotten it.[41] The Danes, lacking Palmerston's sense of humour, took the incorporation of Schleswig into Denmark very seriously. Just as predictably, the German states sought to make Holstein part of the German Confederation. On 30 March 1863, the Danish King escalated tensions by issuing a Patent saying that Holstein could join the Confederation in return for Schleswig's incorporation into Denmark. By clearly violating the 1852 agreement, the Danes provided the Germans and, in particular the wily Bismarck, a pretext for retaliation. On 9 July, the German Federal Diet demanded that the Danish King withdraw his Patent. As the Germans waited for the Danes' reply, Palmerston provocatively warned against any interference in Schleswig. He saw through the Germans' designs, he said, and cryptically assured the Danes that they would not stand alone if threatened by military action.[42] On 13 November 1863, the Danes effectively rejected the Federal Diet's demands by adopting a new constitution incorporating Schleswig. A dynastic struggle ensued when the claim of Christian IX to the throne was challenged by a German-sponsored heir of the House of Oldenburg. Overwhelmed by a wave of impassioned nationalism, the new king, Christian IX, stiffened his position.

Bismarck realized quite perceptively that the Danish crisis provided an opportunity to promote Prussia's bid for leadership in central Europe and eventually the unification of Germany. To that end, he painstakingly cultivated ties with Russia, forced Austria into an alliance for fear of losing her standing in the Germanic Confederation, and threw Napoleon III off guard with hints of territorial compensation on the Rhine. With the continental powers on Bismarck's side, Britain was isolated, permitting Bismarck to have a free hand in Denmark.[43] In rationalizing his invasion of Holstein in January 1864 and the occupation of Schleswig one month later, Bismarck took the high ground by claiming that he was upholding the rights of Duke Christian under the 1852 treaty against the claims of the Danish King. On the other hand, Bismarck's added demand that Denmark recognize the nationalistic yearnings of the duchies' German inhabitants (knowing that the Danes could not comply with this condition) allowed him to ignore the Treaty of London's provision for the inseparability of the two duchies. By ignoring the treaty at this point, he was able to act without any diplomatic strictures on him.[44]

Of course, Bismarck's exploitation of the Danish crisis was facilitated by the lack of an alternative solution, short of an invasion of the duchies. Denmark's inflexibility made diplomatic conciliation virtually impossible, and Britain's inaction, despite words of warning, made them unlikely allies. Initially, Palmerston's strong language of July 1863 directed at Prussia mirrored British public opinion. From the outset of Kaiser Wilhelm I's reign, the Kaiser's anti-parliamentary instincts, his inordinate reliance upon the military, and Bismarck's crude emphasis on blood and iron, were inconsistent with the British image of liberal government. It did not help Bismarck's image when he took the Russian side against the Polish rebels and then made the Danes look like underdogs pitted against Prussian bullies. In contrast, Victoria remained faithful to her Germanic dynastic ties and would not support any Anglo-German confrontation. The blunt language of her confidant, Lord Granville, best conveys the intensity of her Teutonic feeling. He said in August 1863 that 'the Queen is up in her stirrups, very German'.[45] More than Palmerston ever did, she appreciated the intrepid force of German nationalism that impelled Bismarck's adventures and, therefore, she acted as brake against British intervention. So meddlesome was her influence that Palmerston had to remind her in January 1864 that she should defend the nation's interests and not meddle in Germany's particular problems.[46]

On the face of it, Palmerston's initial response to the Danish crisis was consistent with his traditional desire to maintain the balance of power in Europe. It would be a mistake, according to Southgate, to interpret Palmerston's statement of July 1863 as a promise of unilateral aid to Denmark in the event of a Prussian attack. Instead, it is suggested that Palmerston was once again invoking the balance of power formula, requiring multilateral action to redress Europe's equilibrium upset caused by Prussia's armed intervention. Similarly, in raising a hue and cry about Prussia's violation of the 1852 agreement, Palmerston was adhering to the principle that indifference to the sanctity of treaties would substitute force for the rule of law. In other words, 'Might would make right' – making it axiomatic for weaker nations to fall prey to stronger powers. He wasn't just thinking about Prussia, for such a danger could come from France, Russia or Austria. But was the balance of power principle realistically operable in the new age of Bismarckian *Realpolitik*? In the case of Prussia, Palmerston was clear-sighted enough in telling Russell, in December 1863, that 'Schleswig is no part of Germany, and its invasion by German troops would be an act of war versus Denmark, which would in my clear opinion entitle Denmark to our active military and naval support.' In the same breath, he also recognized that such a commitment could not be made without the agreement of the Cabinet or the queen.[47]

Working within these constraints, Palmerston's government could not cope with the heightening crisis in Europe. On 24 December 1863, Holstein was occupied by Austro-Prussian forces, with the invasion of Schleswig following on 1 February. The British government huffed and puffed and Russell spoke of sending the fleet to Copenhagen. This was only talk, for Palmerston cautioned Russell that a land war against the formidable troop strength of Prussia and Austria was a daunting proposition. Even if France were to come to the assistance of Britain, Palmerston feared that Napoleon would exploit the Rhineland mischievously and threaten the status of Belgium and Holland.[48] Not surprisingly, with Denmark still under siege, Russell told the Danes on 19 February that they could not count on assistance from Britain without consultation with Russia and France. However, Anglo-French relations had already been soured by Palmerston's unequivocal rejection of the Emperor's proposal of November 1863. Relations were further strained when the British government failed to prosecute the Italian exile Mazzini who had been implicated in a plot against Napoleon's life. Then when the Italian revolutionary patriot Garibaldi arrived in London to the cheers of the crowd, Paris considered this an affront to the Emperor.[49]

Only a London meeting of the 1852 co-signatories held in April offered any hope for the Danes. At this point, Palmerston's ministry remained divided, the queen continued to rail against anti-German belligerency, and the Tories ridiculed the government for surrendering their role in Europe. News that the Austrian navy was entering the Baltic prompted Russell to send the fleet, but the Cabinet rebuffed him. The conference met from 25 April to 25 June without much effect. Russell got nowhere in recommending a partition of the duchies, and the Germans summarily rejected his recommendation that an arbitrator be chosen. Lacking any other remedy, the conference ended on 25 June with hostilities renewed on the following day. It was cold comfort for the Danes when Russell abjectly responded to their last-minute plea with words of sympathy but still no military assistance. The Danish defeat followed inevitably, as did the Treaty of Vienna of 30 October 1864, by which all of Schleswig–Holstein was surrendered to Austria and Prussia jointly.

The House of Commons met on 27 June to debate the Opposition's motion of censure against the government for their pusillanimous Danish policy. Russell argued that Britain had been forced to choose a neutral course when faced with the prospect of a war in Europe. Disraeli characterized the ministers' policy as one of 'menaces never accomplished and promises never fulfilled'. The radicals joined the Tories in the attack, saying that it would have been better to abandon interventionism altogether in pursuit of a Cobdenite peace. Palmerston, showing his age and infirmity, merely repeated his adherence to the balance of power concept and tried to turn the debate to a discussion of the healthy state of the nation's economy. Such diversions satisfied some, and in the end the censure motion was defeated in the Commons by an amendment, 313 votes to 295.[50]

It has been suggested that this censure motion represented a turning-point in British diplomatic history. It amounted to the abandonment of Palmerston's policy of selective interventionism for one of self-conscious hesitancy in addressing crises around the world.

Palmerston would be criticized for anachronistically believing that he could gain the adherence of the Great Powers in a cynical age of *Realpolitik*. He simply could not cope with Bismarck's opportunistic schemes, ignoring the sanctity of treaties and making alliances for the purpose of breaking them. Palmerston later rationalized Bismarck's victory by welcoming Prussia's new hegemony in central Europe. In the end, he argued that, given the inefficacy of the balance of power system, Europe would benefit from a stronger Prussia. Prussia could act as a sentinel on the Rhine, guarding against French ambitions while also acting as a brake upon Russia's far-flung ventures.[51] These afterthoughts did not explain away his humiliation in 1864, and the vote on the censure motion enforced the impression that Palmerston's days were numbered.

In the months that followed, there were other signs that Palmerston was in decline. Recurrences of gout, intermittent colds and bladder failure plagued him. Absences from Parliament increased, and forgetfulness and dozing on the front bench became routine. His colleagues were in awe that he could go on, while many of his opponents simply bided their time until his departure. Palmerston's association with Garibaldi's visit to London in the spring, which brought out enthusiastic well-wishers, temporarily buoyed up his popularity. Palmerston also used visits to the provinces as a tonic for his recent misfortunes in the House. In June he received an honorary degree at Cambridge; later, he attended the Speech Day festivities at Harrow. Such events, although physically taxing for his octogenarian fame, posed no political danger. Typically, Palmerston followed his opening of a new railway line by making an inoffensive speech filled with platitudes about the state of the nation. Such insipid statements did not appease crowds of working-men in industrial Bradford who confronted Palmerston with demands for franchise reform. Waving flags and polite applause masked the sullen nature of the crowds until radical speakers drew cheers in upbraiding Palmerston.[52] Where was the bumptious politician, who turned aside criticism with self-deprecating humour while reminding his audience of the nation's past glories? This looked like the beginning of the end for Palmerston unless he could rise to the new challenges facing him in Parliament.

In May, the reform issue was revived, when Edward Baines moved to extend the vote to £6 occupiers. Palmerston, who could not attend the debates, advised Gladstone to keep the question open and not commit the ministry to specific measures. Gladstone followed this admonition but later said off-handedly that every man was entitled to come within the pale of the constitution. Behind this statement was the growing belief, shared by John Bright, that British workers personified the virtues of hard work, thrift and commitment to Christian values. Moved by his own religious awakening, Gladstone saw dignity in the lowly and miserable condition of the people. His evangelizing instinct, combined with his desire to unburden workers from a multiplicity of excise taxes, was winning new followers to his side. His rhetoric, however, alienated others with his sense of importance and doctrinal demands.

Palmerston was infuriated by Gladstone's public comments. He thought his Chancellor had deceived him in espousing the doctrine of universal manhood suffrage – namely that every qualified man had the moral right to vote. Palmerston admitted that there were some working-men who were as eligible as any enfranchised 'ten pounders', but he was not ready to give people the suffrage simply because of their class. To Palmerston, Gladstone was provoking workers to agitate for the franchise when the government's duty was to calm the people.[53] Beneath Gladstone's lofty nostrums, he saw vaunting political ambition aimed at reshaping the liberal agenda in a post-Palmerstonian age. Gladstone denied that he was forcing Palmerston's hand or leading a rebellion in the Cabinet. Still, it was a tactical question for Palmerston; there was no need to make general concessions prematurely as this would limit the opportunity to negotiate in the future.[54]

It is easy enough to see this collision between the two men as a struggle between the forces of innovation and reform against the intractable, blind guardians of the past. Steele has argued, however, that this received view of Palmerston, as someone filled with class fear, is an 'inversion of the truth'. Palmerston, he claims, wished to avoid a class war that might disturb the economy and the peaceful transition towards democracy. It is Steele's theory that, unlike the thrust of Gladstone's 11 May speech, Palmerston hoped for the upward mobility of the disenfranchised. He viewed the workers, not as a class separated from those above them, but as individual people who possessed the intelligence and maturity to reach higher goals. In short, he believed that they aspired to rise into the middle classes. Coincidentally, one month before Gladstone's speech, Palmerston voiced similar optimistic sentiments in a speech made in Lambeth. For this he drew criticism from the Tories for holding out unrealistic hopes to the lower orders. Steele believes Palmerston did reach out to the people from the platform and elevated the British self-image more than any other nineteenth-century politician. In a sense, Palmerston's objection to Gladstone's indiscriminant offer of votes to the workers as a class was because he thought too much of them as individual people. Where Gladstone was ambiguous and uncertain in his view of the democratizing process, Palmerston was forceful and clear in recognizing, as John Stuart Mill did, that having the vote was a trust and not a right, which entailed an aristocratic process of gradual improvement. In point of fact, Gladstone, who was surprised at the fuss being made over his remarks, is described by Steele as truly Palmerstonian in his approach to reform. He, too, thought in evolutionary terms, believing that, in order to preserve an elitist structure, public opinion must learn restraint.[55]

This rivalry between the two men appeared yet again in October, as Gladstone prepared his 1865 budget. Gladstone renewed his war of words with Palmerston by returning to the theme of arms reductions. Palmerston's response came in a fusillade of words that amounted to a declarative veto of any proposed cuts in the army estimates. Technological advances in the military had gone too far, he insisted, to be curtailed by budgetary restrictions. The nation's security depended, he said, on these improvements, such as advance in higher calibre cannon, breech-loading rifles and enhanced fortifications. As the new parliamentary session approached, Gladstone knew that in this titanic struggle he lacked the broad support of the Cabinet, saying on 19 January 1865, 'My *opinion* is manifestly in a minority, but there is an unwillingness to have a row.' Palmerston, too, realized that he had again won a major battle over the budget, telling the queen that 'Mr Gladstone is disposed to yield.'[56]

Some observers thought that the 1865 parliamentary session was unusually calm. Palmerston could not last much longer, they reasoned, so why not continue the game of watchful waiting. But it was a calm without repose. There was, as Steele has argued, a myth of inaction surrounding Palmerston's last days. If Palmerston's tongue-in-cheek statement to Lord Goschen is to be believed, the government had sunk into torpor. In answer to Goschen's question about future reforms, Palmerston had responded, 'Oh, there is really nothing to be done. We cannot go on adding to the Statute Book *ad infinitum*. Perhaps we may have a little law reform, or bankruptcy reform; but we cannot go on legislating for ever.'[57] In fact, Palmerston showed no sign of inactivity. He was still in harness, ready to address the issues of the day.

Palmerston's other pre-occupation in these last years was with Ireland. From the time he had inherited his Sligo estates, he had shown his personal sensitivity to the plight of the Irish people, and especially to the impoverished Roman Catholics. As a landlord he had promoted plans for access to education and improvements in the infrastructure, including, harbours and land reclamation. This had been in line with his public policy aimed at integrating British and Irish interests under the 1801 Act of Union. He sought these goals, however, with no illusions about the dangers inherent in Irish revolutionary nationalism. Comparisons of Anglo-Irish relations to Britain's tenuous authority in India after 1857 were vivid in his mind whenever he assessed the future loss of Ireland to the empire.[58] As in India, Britain faced the dilemma of conciliating the aggrieved without tolerating acts of terrorism. When violence again erupted in Ireland in 1861, his Parliamentary Secretary, Henry Brand, reminded him, 'Is it wise in the present state of Europe to inflame Ireland?' Later, Brand drove home the point when he told Palmerston, 'The day may not be very distant where we may have to call upon the loyalty of Irishmen.' Implicit in such warnings was the knowledge that a third of the British army consisted of Irish Catholics. Using them against mutinous Indians may not have raised questions, but to send them to Canada, a refuge for Fenian rebels, was another matter.[59]

From Palmerston's perspective, the major obstacle to winning the Irish people's loyalty was the Irish Catholic Church which was both nationalistic and committed to the papacy. It would do no good to conciliate Irish Catholics, he thought, if priests and bishops indoctrinated the people to oppose Protestantism.[60] He was, therefore, reluctant to support a separate Catholic university, which might become an island of orthodoxy. Similarly, so long as the Pope enjoyed spiritual and temporal sovereignty in Rome, he commanded the loyalty of the Irish faithful and competed politically with Westminster.

Although Palmerston failed to draw Irish Catholics away from their faith, he contributed, albeit marginally, to ameliorating their wretched status as tenants. Although his glib maxim 'Tenant right is landlord wrong' has stigmatized him as a callous absentee landlord, his true position deserves re-examination. Typically, the English absentee landlord has been characterized as one who forced his tenants to make uncompensated improvements, so as to realize greater profits from the land. To make matters worse, tenants were faced with the burden of rack-renting and the prospect of eviction when payments fell into arrears. Given this historic picture of injustice, Irish Catholics saw it as their 'right' to seek remedies from their perceived grievances. Indeed, it could be argued that since the famine of 1845–7 evictions and the resultant emigrations had only accelerated and deepened the tenants' misery. Palmerston's response to this process of deterioration was to recognize publicly the abysmal condition of the Irish and place it in historical context. He readily recited the litany of wrongs perpetuated against the Irish, including confiscations, penal laws, and the hegemony of the Protestant minority over the Catholic majority. His response was to allow his tenants to become almost sole proprietors of their holdings by sale or inheritance. Moreover, compensation for improvements to the land became routine practice on his Irish estates.[61] As a matter of public policy, however, his high regard for the sanctity of private property kept him from supporting a statue enforcing such compensation or 'tenant right'. This would be confiscatory, he thought, since it violated the natural rights of property. Such a concession would capitulate to Irish terrorism and jeopardize the lives of landlords and Protestants.[62] Although he wanted to produce an integrated union of educated, law-abiding, Catholic and Protestant citizens, he was not yet prepared to do so at the expense of the traditional landed class.

Different from, but related to, Palmerston's treatment of Irish Catholics was the mark he left upon the established Church of England. Although a nominal Anglican, he took seriously his responsibility to oversee the Church of England as prime minister. Overall, he wanted religion to ameliorate rather than strain class relations. Because Anglicanism was tied to the state, Protestant dissent was viewed warily as a source of agitation, especially over such thorny issues as church rates, educational reform and freedom of religion. Given the divisions between Anglican high and low churchmen, Palmerston crafted a sophisticated policy that responded to the varying needs of these groups while maintaining religious solidarity and social stability. In particular, he was sensitive to the skilled labourers, who aspired to be part of the burgeoning middle class. By reaching out to the dissenters amongst them, he provided an access route for civic and religious improvements without the necessity of expanding the franchise. He was reluctant to accede to the radicals' demand for the vote, but he could provide a sense of inclusion by relieving religious disabilities and thereby unite them with the national church. To do this he forged relations with key individuals who spoke the language of dissent better than he did. Palmerston's warm relationship with the evangelical Earl of Shaftesbury, undoubtedly influenced the reshaping of the Anglican episcopate between 1855 and 1865. In his ten years as prime minister, Palmerston appointed 21 men to English bishoprics as well as several to the Irish Established Church. At his death, more than half of the English bishops were his appointees. Given the Shaftesbury connection and Palmerston's inclination to adopt a broad church position, it was not surprising that these clergy were tolerant of dissenting views.[63] These episcopal appointments reflected Palmerston's own desire that a doctrine of practical Christianity be preached to meet the needs of the ordinary man. He wanted bishops who were skilled administrators and pastoral preachers but who did not assume intellectual airs with their flocks. It did not matter to Palmerston that his bishops lacked academic credentials since he distrusted the Church divines whose sermons were steeped in theory rather than good sense. It suited him as well that his bishops were adverse to ritualism because of its suggestive links with Rome which alienated the people from the Church.[64]

Palmerston's choice of measures and men also evinced his use of religious policy to reach out to dissenters. In addition to finding an ally in Lord Shaftesbury, he developed links with Edward Baines, the dissenting editor of the *Leeds Mercury* and a leading figure in the reform-minded Liberation Society. His newspaper had supported Palmerston during the Crimean War and had recognized that Palmerston's bellicosity was not so repugnant that he would lose public support. Baines, unlike more acerbic radical critics such as John Bright, believed in making overtures to enlightened aristocrats who held that change was compatible with the maintenance of a well-ordered society. While disclaiming any intention of damaging the Church establishment, Baines became Palmerston's conduit for religious reform. Beginning in 1855, he became the foremost exponent of abolishing Church rates. Repeatedly passed by the House of Commons but stymied by the Lords, it finally won passage in 1868. His influence was also behind the effort to diminish the Anglican monopoly over education by supporting the Endowed Schools Act of 1860, which declared that Anglican grammar schools should be open to dissenting pupils.[65]

Parliament was dissolved on 7 July 1865, allowing an enfeebled Palmerston to meet his Tiverton constituents on the hustings. It was a quiet election as controversial issues receded into the background. There appeared to be no basis for any direct attack on Palmerston. Instead, the theme of class harmony dominated most speeches. Certainly, there were allusions to parliamentary reform, religious change and peace abroad but within the optimistic context that nothing was insoluble in this enlightened age. Those radicals who continued their calls for parliamentary reform had been silenced by the assumption among many that it would come in its own good time. Meanwhile, the wind had been taken out of the Opposition's sails, leaving the Tories on the defensive. Under Derby in the 1850s they responded to Palmerston's popularity with the passive strategy of watchful waiting. Now in 1865, Palmerston's election victory was taken for granted. Disraeli's inability to exploit the Schleswig–Holstein question sent a signal to the electorate that Palmerston was invincible. There were some rumblings about the divisions in the Cabinet and Palmerston's inability to discipline his ranks, but as men like Gladstone and Russell fell in line, they soon died down. The only contentious question that arose in the campaign was Palmerston himself and the furtherance of his policy of pragmatic liberalism. His gift to the nation, especially in his second ministry, was his openness to moderate radicalism, circumscribed by a continuing belief in aristocratic government. Never courting revolution or reaction, Palmerstonianism could best be described in evolutionary terms.

The 1865 election results amounted to a clear-cut vote of confidence in Palmerston. The Liberals gained 60.2% of the vote in contrast to the Conservative vote of 39.8%. This translated into an increase from 356 seats in the House of Commons in 1859 to 369 seats in 1865, while the Tories declined from 298 in 1859 to 289 in 1865. Along with consolidating their base in England, the Liberals also made gains in Scotland, Wales and Ireland. Palmerston won easily in Tiverton.[66]

In an attempt to recuperate from the campaign's rigours before the next Parliamentary session started, Palmerston retreated to Brocket Hall, the ancestral home of Lady Palmerston. There, he prepared his agenda for the coming session while nursing a cold and his other chronic maladies. There is no evidence that Palmerston was about to leave office and much less quit politics. As death approached he was still to be found at his desk, dealing with such mundane matters as allowing half-day Saturday work schedules for civil servants. His cold led to a fever and then, complicated by high blood pressure, kidney failure followed. He died on Wednesday, 18 October 1865, age 81, feebly mouthing references to parts of the Belgian Treaty.[67]

Conclusion

Many of the eulogies for Palmerston in 1865 spoke glowingly of his place in history. Gladstone's comment that 'Death has indeed laid low the most towering antlers in all the forest',[1] testified to Palmerston's impact on his age. The question remains, however, what was that influence and how do we assess it? As indicated at the outset of this study, the caricature of Palmerston as the crude John Bull of nineteenth-century Britain, practising gunboat diplomacy abroad and obstructing reform at home, no longer suffices as a definition of the man. More accurately, historians are left with a paradoxical figure whose long and complicated life lends itself to varied interpretations. Just like the times he personified, he represented conflicting points of view.

Palmerston's eighteenth-century aristocratic origins only partially explain his attitude towards reform. His commitment to the aristocracy's privileges and inherent political power was steadfast, and based on the belief that the wholesale extension of such rights to the public was fraught with danger. His insistent quarrel with Russell over widening the franchise in the 1850s and 1860s was based on his belief that Britain's balanced constitution would be threatened by an encroaching democracy. While Palmerston was not afraid to cultivate the crowd's support, he had a healthy suspicion of their capacity to act responsibly. This did not mean he was an opponent of reform, as can be testified by his early support for Catholic emancipation and the abolition of the slave trade. Moreover, even as an apprentice minister in the War Office, it was clear that he was a man of action who believed that the government had a role to play in serving the best interests of the nation. Throughout his years in office he worked himself and his department hard in an effort to serve his nation's interests to the best of his ability. Investigating abuses in the army, fostering educational reforms, and sponsoring public health measures were all marked by efficient and fair administrative practices, a harbinger of governmental modernization. Wedded to his commitment to efficient government was Palmerston's belief that the nation's security required the state to play a larger role in raising taxes for necessary military expenditures. At the same time, Palmerston's Liberal governments pleased the public by demonstrating that, just as they could raise revenue for the nation, their prudent efficiencies also allowed them to reduce taxes. In short, while Palmerston understood the appropriate limits on government, he reconciled his *laissez faire* views with an awareness of the growing power of the state. In creating a new type of Liberal government and then manning it with a refashioned Liberal Party, Palmerston shifted from his aristocratic underpinnings to his embrace of nineteenth-century modernity.

Just as it would be difficult for some to recast Palmerston as a modernizing reformer, it would be hard to dispel the image of him as a bull mastiff in foreign affairs. A superficial view of him would suggest that the same man who displayed leadership, a true man of action, could also be described as impulsive, and, at best, improvisational in his conduct of foreign policy. Few could disagree that Palmerston exhibited these assertive characteristics in his first term at the Foreign Office when he significantly turned Castlereagh's policy of non-interventionism on its head in Portugal and Spain. His interventions in both countries announced to the world that gunboat diplomacy was an instrument of British foreign policy. Similarly, it could be argued that, in approaching the brink of war with France in 1840 over the Mehemet Ali crisis, he risked alienating an essential member of the Quadruple Alliance. Palmerston's testy relations with the United States and his reliance on force to deal with crises in China and India also troubled his more cautious critics at court and in parliament. Of course, championing Don Pacifico and later his identification with the Crimean War were the high points of his international adventurism.

Taken by itself, however, this caricature provides only a limited view of the man. Unlike George Canning, Palmerston was not a deeply thoughtful intellectual with a profound vision of the future. He was a man of action and energy who seized opportunities to serve his nation's interests and broadcast their achievements. He pursued these ends not thoughtlessly but through a framework of ideas. Although he might be charged with not understanding the long-term significance of certain events (his reaction to the 1848 revolutions comes to mind), he did anchor his actions in the pursuit of certain fundamental goals. He understood quite clearly the connection between the achievement of national prosperity, world trade, and the maintenance of peace and stability. The furtherance of these ends would be best facilitated, he thought, in constitutionally liberal states with a strong middle class generating progressive achievements for its people. In asserting that such states were Britain's natural allies, he realized that, given the divided interests of the Great Powers, the 1815 Vienna settlement alone would not guarantee peace and stability. An alliance system, roughly falling along an east–west divide, was necessary in order to maintain Europe's balance of power.

Following this line of thought, a cautious diplomat emerged who tempered his assertive diplomacy with scrupulous attention to detail and the use of adroit negotiating skills. The achievement of Belgium's independence comes to mind. Here, despite his relative inexperience as a diplomat, Palmerston caught the attention of the courts of Europe for skilfully coaxing the Great Powers to overcome their differences and guarantee Belgium's sovereignty. His victories for constitutionalism in Lisbon and Madrid were due less to his belligerency and more to his deft inclusion of France in the Quadruple Alliance, as a guarantor of Spain and Portugal's independence. Although his words of encouragement for Italian liberals angered Victoria, higher on his agenda was his concern that France might foment strife with Austria. Indeed, his overall sympathy for the 1848 revolutions was contingent on avoiding threats to the peace of Europe. Therefore, while he urged the Hapsburgs to promote reform in Lombardy and Venetia, he feared that Austria would invite instability in central Europe.

There were also natural limits to Palmerston's diplomatic boldness. Although it has been said that he was a bully to the weak and a coward to the strong, it meant that he used force when it was likely to succeed and avoided unwise confrontations. He attacked Greece, China and India with impunity but thought twice about sending troops to Poland, Italy or Germany. It was Palmerston's ambiguous relationship with France that best exemplifies his brand of diplomacy. While it was becoming increasingly obvious that France could be viewed as Britain's natural rival, Palmerston treated the French with a velvet glove more than the mailed fist. While always suspicious of Louis Philippe's intentions, he used the Quadruple Alliance as both a bond of friendship and a restraint on French ambitions. He viewed Napoleon III's designs on Italy and the Rhineland with trepidation, but risked losing office to defend his interests in 1852 and 1858. Palmerston's calculated retreats may raise questions about his control over events, especially in his last years, as balance of power politics gave way to Bismarckian bellicosity, but at least it demonstrated the pragmatic nature of his diplomacy.

Palmerston's over-riding occupation with diplomacy did not mean he was indifferent to the party politics of his day. Having served in government from 1809 almost continuously until his death in 1865, he became a power broker who influenced political alliances, the formation of Cabinets, and the articulation of party policy. On the face of it, in tracking his different political incarnations (from his early years as a Canningite, to his emergence as a Whig, his flirtations with Derbyites and radicals, culminating in his leadership of the Liberal Party) it is difficult to assign Palmerston any political identity. Given this chameleon-like political history, one is inclined to place him above party, away from the divisions and in-fighting that so characterized the period from 1846 to 1855. In this way, it was possible to say that if he did not represent a particular party, he did speak for the people at large. It also means that, as the Tories and Whigs searched to find agreement on issues such as free trade and parliamentary reform, Palmerston found new ways to rally the public behind him. He did so by not concentrating on what divided people so much as what united them. According to Steele, instead of hardening class divisions, Palmerston tried to mend them. Rising above parties, he elevated the public's consciousness to its achievements at mid-century. Britain's national prosperity, its technical and cultural progress and, most importantly, its growth as a liberal and enlightened society were emblazoned chauvinistically before the public as an icon for their appreciation. Appealing to the public's self-congratulatory nature, he seized the moral high ground in proclaiming that Britain had set the standard for the world. It was only fair, he argued that the British people share their bounty with those people who wished to shed despotism's yoke for the experience of enlightened liberalism. By diverting the people's attention abroad he effectively kept their minds off pressing reform issues. Here, at least, Palmerston's words, assiduously propagated by a well-cultivated press, counted for more than his actions. Surpassing his political rivals, Palmerston was ahead of his time in reading the public's mind and in daring to speak for it to the world. In doing so, he marginalized his radical critics by breaking their monopoly over morality. Instead, by reconciling Britain's pursuit of its own interests abroad with the mission to propagate constitutionalism, he gave the people a higher patriotic calling.

Conclusion

To say that Palmerston acted above party by going directly to the people did not preclude him from being a party man. Indeed, his place in government would be inexplicable without his party connections. As ministries were fashioned from an array of parties, Whigs, Derbyites, Peelites among them, Palmerston's name figured prominently among those under consideration. To be sure, his attraction lay in his indispensability as a magnet for popular support. But his views were also conveniently compatible with those from different sides of Parliament. He received support from patriotic radicals such as John Roebuck while old Peelites agreed with him on free trade. Tory evangelicals were happy with his episcopal appointments and cautious middle-class liberals joined him in supporting a circumscribed parliamentary reform bills. Palmerston's talent was in knowing, more than Russell or Gladstone did, that the nation was unprepared for extreme change in an age of equipoise. He was able to reconcile divergent interests to produce a consensus that represented the nation's will. This meant pulling together the constituent parts of the future Liberal Party which fostered freedom protected by order, government intrusion without abandoning individual accountability, and military security, checked by budgetary discipline, all under aristocratic leaders who were accessible to the people. That was the accomplishment realized at Willis's Room meeting of 1858 and incarnated in the second Palmerston ministry.

To describe the mid-Victorian age as Palmerstonian suggests that his impact extended beyond the world of politics. If his name was synonymous with the age then perhaps he also personified the nation and its people. The measure of that proposition may lie less in the man himself, his bumptious style, his optimism and his enthusiam for hard work, although this was how he charmed the people. Rather, it may be found in his instinctive understanding of the British populace at mid-century and the manner in which he translated that understanding to the wider nineteenth-century world. Palmerston perceived that the British people had rallied around a unifying principle that was not social class, nor was it solely religion or a single party. It was nationalism. By elevating the public's awareness to what it meant to be British – that is, to its traditions, its liberal values, its economic and cultural accomplishments, its power and most importantly, its moral contribution to the world's betterment – Palmerston defined the group ideal. Palmerston combined his healthy distrust of the crowd's capacity for self-governance with a growing respect for its power. This ambivalent attitude meant that he preferred to speak to, and for, the people, rather than be driven by them. But he was not simply a demagogue whose survival depended on the masses. Palmerston was sustained in office by parliamentary elections producing majorities in the House of Commons and not by plebiscites. Still, he was far-sighted enough to know that by using the manipulative powers of the press, he could shape the thinking of an increasingly literate public and move them to follow his lead. In short, he anticipated the coming of democracy by trying to curtail its excesses. In doing so, he spoke for his times but with an eye to the future.

NOTES

Chapter 1: The Making of a Canningite

1. Kenneth Bourne, *Palmerston: The Early Years, 1784–1841* (New York: Macmillan, 1982) pp. 59, 60; Jasper Ridley, *Lord Palmerston* (New York: E. P. Dutton, 1971) p. 22; *Hansard's Parliamentary Debates*, n. s. XIV, 919 [hereafter cited as *Hansard*].
2. Bourne, *Palmerston*, pp. 78, 79; Ridley, *Lord Palmerston*, p. 27.
3. Sir H. L. Bulwer (Lord Dalling and Bulwer), *The Life of Henry John Temple, Viscount Palmerston, with Selections from his Diaries and Correspondence*, 3 vols (London: R. Bentley, 1870–4) vol. I, pp. 81–3 [hereafter cited as Bulwer]; Kenneth Bourne (ed.), *The Letters of the Third Viscount Palmerston to Laurence and Elizabeth Sulivan, 1804–1863*, Camden 4th series, vol. XXIII (London: Royal Historical Society, 1979) p. 99 [hereafter cited as Sulivan].
4. *Hansard*, n.s. X, 300, 301.
5. Palmerston to Malmesbury, 15 October 1809, Bulwer, vol. I, p. 89; Bourne, *Palmerston*, p. 85.
6. Bulwer, vol. I, pp. 90–5; Bourne, *Palmerston*, p. 86.
7. Palmerston to Malmesbury, 16 October 1809, in the 3rd Earl Malmesbury (ed.), *Malmesbury Letters: A Series of Letters of the First Earl of Malmesbury and his Family and Friends, from 1745 to 1820* (London: R. Bentley, 1870) vol. II, pp. 155–7 [hereafter *Malmesbury Letters*]; Bulwer, vol. I, pp. 92–4.
8. Ridley, *Lord Palmerston*, p. 35.
9. Palmerston to Malmesbury, 16 October 1809, in *Malmesbury Letters*, vol. II, p. 156.
10. H. F. C. Bell, *Lord Palmerston*, vol. I (London: Longmans, Green, 1870) p. 18 [hereafter cited as Bell].
11. Donald Southgate, *'The Most English Minister...': The Policies and Politics of Palmerston* (London: Macmillan, 1966) p. 3; Bourne, *Palmerston*, pp. 86, 87; Ridley, *Lord Palmerston*, pp. 34–5.
12. Bourne, *Palmerston*, pp. 98, 99.
13. Ibid.; Ridley, *Lord Palmerston*, p. 36.

14. Bourne, *Palmerston*, p. 162.
15. Palmerston's memorandum to the Prince Regent, 16 August 1811, BL Add. MS 48417; Bulwer, vol. I, pp. 384–417.
16. Bourne, *Palmerston*, pp. 172, 177.
17. Palmerston to his sister Fanny, 27 February 1810, Bulwer, vol. I, pp. 115–16; Bourne, *Palmerston*, pp. 133, 134.
18. *Hansard*, XXXIII, 995, 1001, 1002; Ridley, *Lord Palmerston*, p. 55.
19. *Hansard*, XXI, 1202, 1281–3; Ridley, *Lord Palmerston*, pp. 49, 50.
20. Ibid., pp. 64, 66, 67; Bulwer, vol. I, pp. 83, 84.
21. *Hansard*, n.s., VI, 309–13; Ridley, *Lord Palmerston*, p. 69.
22. Palmerston's *Autobiography*, Broadlands Papers, PP/D/26.
23. Ridley, *Lord Palmerston*, 83; Palmerston's *Autobiography*, Broadlands Papers, PP/D/26.
24. Palmerston's *Autobiography*, Broadlands Papers, PP/D/26; Bulwer, vol. I, pp. 371–2; Ridley, *Lord Palmerston*, pp. 42–4, 83, 84.
25. Michael Bentley, *Politics without Democracy, 1815–1914: Perceptions and Preoccupations in British Government* (London: Fontana Press, 1996) p. 57.
26. R. W. Seton-Watson, *Britain in Europe, 1789–1914: A Survey of Foreign Policy* (Cambridge: Cambridge University Press, 1955) p. 71.
27. *Hansard*, n.s., VIII, 885–9, 894, 1514.
28. Seton-Watson, *Britain in Europe*, pp. 84–6; Asa Briggs, *The Age of Improvement, 1783–1867* (London: Longmans, Green, 1959) pp. 347, 348.
29. Palmerston to his sister Elizabeth, Broadlands Papers, PP/D/26; Bulwer, vol. I, pp. 85–8; Sulivan, p. 175, note 2.
30. Sulivan, pp. 79, 80.
31. *Hansard*, XXIV, 971–6; Bourne, *Palmerston*, p. 230.
32. Palmerston to Devonshire, 5 June 1825, Bourne, *Palmerston*, p. 242.
33. *Hansard*, n.s., XIII, 558–62. For a detailed discussion of the Cabinet's position between 1821 and 1829 see Richard W. Davis, 'Wellington and the "Open Question": the Issue of Catholic Emancipation, 1821–1829', *Albion*, 29: 1 (Spring 1997) pp. 39–55.
34. Davis, 'Wellington and the "Open Question"', p. 46.
35. Palmerston to William Temple, 4 December 1825, Bulwer, vol. I, pp. 164–8.
36. Palmerston to William Temple, 5 June 1826, Bulwer, vol. I, pp. 167–72; Ridley, *Lord Palmerston*, p. 87; Bourne, *Palmerston*, p. 247.
37. Palmerston to Sulivan, 20 December 1825, Sulivan, pp. 176–8.
38. *Hansard*, n.s., XIV, 919; Ridley, *Lord Palmerston*, pp. 79, 81.
39. Seton-Watson, *Britain in Europe*, p. 68; Briggs, *The Age of Improvement*, p. 220.
40. Briggs, *The Age of Improvement*, p. 226; Bentley, *Politics without Democracy*, p. 67.

41. Canning to Palmerston, 10 June 1827, and Palmerston to Canning, 14 June 1827, Palmerston's *Autobiography*, Broadlands Papers, PP/D/26, Sulivan, p. 187.
42. *Hansard*, n.s., XVII, 302, 303; Ridley, *Lord Palmerston*, pp. 89–91; Bourne, *Palmerston*, pp. 253–64.
43. Bulwer, vol. I, p. 191.
44. Muriel E. Chamberlain, *Lord Palmerston* (Washington, DC: Catholic University Press, 1987) p. 35.
45. Arthur Aspinall, 'The Formation of the Goderich Ministry', *English Historical Review*, XLII (1927) pp. 533–59.
46. Davis, 'Wellington and the "Open Question"', pp. 39–55.
47. Palmerston to William Temple, 18 January 1828, Bulwer, vol. I, pp. 215–20; Bourne, *Palmerston*, p. 276.
48. Palmerston to William Temple, 18 January 1828, Bulwer, vol. I, pp. 217–20.
49. Palmerston's *Journal*, 28 March 1828, Broadlands Papers, PP/D/2; Bulwer, vol. I, pp. 239–46; Bourne, *Palmerston*, p. 277; Ridley, *Lord Palmerston*, p. 95.
50. Palmerston to William Temple, 8 May 1828, Bulwer, vol. I, pp. 225–8.
51. *Hansard*, n.s., XIX, 538, 962–70, 1217; Palmerston to William Temple, 22 May 1828, Palmerston to Wellington, 25 May 1828, Wellington to Palmerston, 26 May 1828, all in Bulwer, vol. I, pp. 253–76.
52. *Hansard*, n.s., XIX, 538.
53. Quoted in Ridley, *Lord Palmerston*, p. 97.
54. Bentley, *Politics without Democracy*, p. 74; Briggs, *Age of Improvement*, p. 232.
55. *Hansard*, n.s., XX, 235, 1237–53.
56. *Hansard*, n.s., XXI, 1643–70.
57. *Hansard*, n.s., XXI, 1643–70; Southgate, 'The Most English Minister', pp. 8–13; Chamberlain, *Lord Palmerston*, p. 40.
58. Palmerston to Sulivan, 7 October 1829, Sulivan, p. 235. See also B.T. Bradfield, 'Sir Richard Vyvyan and the Fall of the Wellington Government', *Historical Journal*, XI (1968) pp. 141–56.
59. A. Mitchell, *The Whigs in Opposition, 1815–1830* (Oxford: Clarendon Press, 1967) pp. 230, 231.
60. Ibid., pp. 232, 233; Eric Evans, *The Forging of the Modern State: Early Industrial Britain, 1783–1870*, 2nd edn (London: Longman, 1996) Appendix B, p. 404.
61. 3 *Hansard*, I, 52, 53.
62. Palmerston's *Autobiography*, Broadlands Papers, PP/D/26; Ridley, *Lord Palmerston*, p. 104.
63. Ridley, *Lord Palmerston*, pp. 104, 105.
64. Stuart Reid (ed.), *Durham: The Life and Letters of the First Earl Durham, 1792–1840* (London: Longmans, Green, 1906) vol. I, p. 216; Sulivan, pp. 247, 248; Bourne, *Palmerston*, p. 329.

Chapter 2: Interests but No Entanglements

1. Seton-Watson, *Britain in Europe*, p. 156.
2. Palmerston to Sir John, Viscount Ponsonby, 1 December 1830, BL Add. MS 48446.
3. Southgate, *'The Most English Minister'*, p. 30.
4. Ridley, *Lord Palmerston*, p. 127.
5. Ibid., p. 130.
6. Palmerston to the 1st Earl Granville, 2 February 1831, Bulwer, vol. II, p. 38 and notes 42–3.
7. Southgate, *'The Most English Minister'*, p. 34; Ridley, *Lord Palmerston*, p. 131.
8. Ridley, *Lord Palmerston*, p. 131.
9. Palmerston to Granville, 17 May 1831, BL Add. MS 48543.
10. Palmerston to Sir Charles Bagot, 27 June 1831, BL Add. MS 48466.
11. 3 *Hansard*, V, 661, 880, 881, 1209–14, 1270–1310.
12. Bulwer, vol. II, p. 105, 109; Ridley, *Lord Palmerston*, p. 135.
13. Ridley, *Lord Palmerston*, p. 136.
14. Quoted in Southgate, *'The Most English Minister'*, pp. 36–7.
15. C. K. Webster, *Foreign Policy of Palmerston, 1830–1841: Britain, the Liberal Movement and the Eastern Question* (London: G. Bell, 1951), vol. I, p. 145 [hereafter cited as Webster].
16. 3 *Hansard*, XIV, 1162–5.
17. Palmerston to Charles Grant, Lord Glenelg, 17 August 1830, in Webster, vol. I, pp. 80, 81; Southgate, *'The Most English Minister'*, pp. 26–8.
18. Palmerston to Granville, 11 March 1831, Bulwer, vol. II, pp. 50–1.
19. Palmerston to Taylor, 2 April 1831 and 22 June 1831, BL Add. MS 48470.
20. Seton-Watson, *Britain in Europe*, p. 170.
21. Southgate, *'The Most English Minister'*, p. 45.
22. Webster, vol. I, p. 211; Bourne, *Palmerston*, p. 366.
23. Ridley, *Lord Palmerston*, p. 141; 3 *Hansard*, VI, 1218; Seton-Watson, *Britain in Europe*, p. 179.
24. George W. Chad to Palmerston, 12 June 1831, BL Add. MS 48481.
25. 3 *Hansard*, VI, 1218; Seton-Watson, *Britain in Europe*, pp. 179–80.
26. 3 *Hansard*, IX, 963–8; Ridley, *Lord Palmerston*, p. 155; Webster, vol. I, pp. 150–1.
27. Prince Adam Czartoryski, *Memoirs of Prince Adam Czartoryski*, ed. A. Guilgud (New York: Arno Press, 1971) vol. II, pp. 339–4.
28. Palmerston to Frederick Lamb, 3 August 1832, Webster, vol. I, p. 229, note.
29. 3 *Hansard*, XIV, 1045–9; Webster, vol. I, p. 229.
30. Palmerston to Frederick Lamb, 3 August 1832, Webster, vol. I, p. 230, note.
31. 3 *Hansard*, XIV, 1045–9; Webster, vol. I, p. 229.
32. Palmerston to Frederick Lamb, 7 September 1832, BL Add. MS 48444.
33. Webster, vol. I, pp. 233–4; Bourne, *Palmerston*, p. 371.

34. Palmerston to Frederick Lamb, 6 April 1833, Webster, vol. I, pp. 357–8.
35. Southgate, 'The Most English Minister', pp. 51–2; Ridley, Lord Palmerston, p. 156.
36. Palmerston to Frederick Lamb, 28 April 1833, Webster, vol. I, p. 235; Southgate, 'The Most English Minister', pp. 54–8.
37. Bulwer, vol. I, pp. 380–3; Ridley, Lord Palmerston, p. 104.
38. 3 Hansard, II, 1318–30.
39. Palmerston to Grey, 8 April 1831, Grey Papers, Department of Palaeography, University of Durham; Bourne, Palmerston, p. 505.
40. Ridley, Lord Palmerston, p. 149.
41. Ibid., p. 150.
42. Palmerston to William Temple, 16 November 1834, Bulwer, vol. II, pp. 207–8; Ridley, Lord Palmerston, p. 181; Southgate, 'The Most English Minister', p. 82.
43. Angus Hawkins, British Party Politics, 1852–1886 (Basingstoke: Palgrave Macmillan, 1998) p. 26.
44. Ridley, Lord Palmerston, pp. 151–4.
45. Ibid., p. 151.
46. Palmerston to Brougham, 9 May 1834, Brougham Papers, University College, London University; Bourne, Palmerston, p. 528.
47. Palmerston to Lady Holland, 7 December 1834, BL ADD. MS 51600; Bourne, Palmerston, p. 540.
48. Southgate, 'The Most English Minister', p. 10; Ridley, Lord Palmerston, p. 99.
49. Southgate, Lord Palmerston, pp. 92–3.
50. Hansard, n.s. XXI, 1643–70.
51. Southgate, 'The Most English Minister', p. 10; Ridley, Lord Palmerston, p. 99.
52. Hansard, n.s. XXIII, 76, 77.
53. Palmerston to Hoppner, 14 January 1831, BL Add. MS 48475.
54. Bulwer, vol. II, pp. 180, 186.
55. Quoted in Seton-Watson, Britain in Europe, p. 190.
56. Southgate, 'The Most English Minister', pp. 5, 6.
57. Ibid., pp. 64–5.
58. Ibid., p. 66.
59. Palmerston to Melbourne, 5 July 1840, Bulwer, vol. II, pp. 356–61; Ridley, Lord Palmerston, p. 233. In addition to the criticism from Francophile Whigs, a campaign was started by David Urquhart, a recently dismissed attaché in Constantinople, alleging that Palmerston had been a Russian spy. Driven more by revenge than reason, the embittered Urquhart relentlessly harassed Palmerston with these charges for twenty years. See Broadlands Papers, PP/FO/H/70–3.
60. Ridley, Lord Palmerston, pp. 258–9. See also Parliamentary Papers, Opium Papers, XXXVI.575, mf. 43.269–70.
61. Eric Evans, The Forging of the Modern State, p. 261.

62. Ridley, *Lord Palmerston*, p. 281; J. Vincent and M. Stinton (eds), *McCalmont's Parliamentary Poll Book: British Election Results, 1832–1918*, 8th edn (Brighton: Harvester Press, 1971) p. 294; Ridley, *Lord Palmerston*, p. 281.

Chapter 3: The Revolutionary Challenge

1. For a full treatment of Palmerston's relationship with the press, see Stephen Koss, *The Rise and Fall of the Political Press in Britain*, vol. 1: *The Nineteenth Century* (Chapel Hill: University of North Carolina Press, 1981).
2. Nicholas Edsel, *Richard Cobden* (Cambridge, Mass.: Harvard University Press, 1986) pp. 108, 151.
3. A. C. Benson and Viscount Esher (eds), *The Letters of Queen Victoria: A Selection of Her Majesty's Correspondence between 1837 and 1861* (London: John Murray, 1908) vol. I, pp. 346–7 [hereafter cited as *Victoria's Letters*]; Ridley, p. 277.
4. Ridley, *Lord Palmerston*, p. 289.
5. 3 *Hansard*, LXX, 1452–93; Palmerston to William Temple, 5 January 1844, Bulwer, vol. III, p. 64.
6. Koss, *Political Press*, p. 76.
7. 3 *Hansard*, LXVII, 1162–1285.
8. 3 *Hansard*, LXIV, 937, 1008, LXV, 1097.
9. 3 *Hansard*, LXXII, 1645, 1646.
10. 3 *Hansard*, LXXXII, 142, 143.
11. For a detailed study of Palmerston's response to famine conditions in Sligo, see Tyler Anbinder, 'Lord Palmerston and the Irish Famine Emigration', *The Historical Journal*, XLIV: 2 (2001) pp. 441–69.
12. Palmerston to Pakenham, 31 March 1847, BL Add. MS 48575.
13. Anbinder, 'Lord Palmerston', p. 453; R. D. Edwards and T. D Williams (eds), *The Great Famine: Studies in Irish History, 1845–1852* (New York: New York University Press, 1956) p. 338.
14. Anbinder, 'Lord Palmerston', pp. 464–7.
15. Bell, *Lord Palmerston*, vol. I, pp. 353–9.
16. Bulwer, vol. III, pp. 192–3; Princess Lieven to Lord Aberdeen, 29 April 1846, and Lord Aberdeen to Princess Lieven, 5 May 1846, E. Parry Jones (ed.), *The Correspondence of Lord Aberdeen to Princess Lieven, 1832–1854*, Camden, 3rd series, vol. LX (London: Royal Historical Society, 1938) vol. I, pp. 249–50.
17. Roman Golicz, 'Napoleon III, Lord Palmerston and the *Entente Cordiale*', *History Today*, vol. 12 (December 2000) p. 11.
18. Palmerston to Bulwer, 19 July 1846, PRO/FO/694.
19. 3 *Hansard*, XCIII, 121–5, 383–467, 472–629, 657–66.
20. *The Times*, 2 August 1847; Ridley, *Lord Palmerston*, pp. 324–5.
21. Southgate, *'The Most English Minister'*, p. 24.

22. Ridley, *Lord Palmerston*, p. 331.
23. Southgate, '*The Most English Minister*', p. 202.
24. Palmerston to Ponsonby, 11 September 1847, PRO/FO/07/335.
25. Palmerston to Normanby, 27 February 1848, BL Add. MS 48455; Victoria to Palmerston, 8 August 1848, in B. Connell (ed.), *Regina v. Palmerston: The Correspondence between Queen Victoria and her Foreign and Prime Minister, 1837–65* (London: Evans, 1902) p. 91.
26. Palmerston to Normanby, 28 February 1848, Bulwer, vol. IV, pp. 81–2.
27. Parliament to Ponsonby, 29 February 1848, BL Add. MS 48547, and Palmerston to Bloomfield, 29 February 1848, BL Add. MS 48563.
28. Palmerston to Normanby, 28 June 1848, BL Add. MS 48555.
29. Palmerston to Ponsonby, 30 June 1848, BL Add. MS 48555.
30. Palmerston to Victoria, 22 May 1848, and Victoria to Palmerston, 21 and 22 May 1848, in Connell, *Regina v. Palmerston*, p. 74.
31. Palmerston to Normanby, 9 March 1849, *Parliamentary Papers, Italian Papers*, LVII. 707, mf. 53.436–8.
32. Seton-Watson, *Britain in Europe*, pp. 265–6.
33. Palmerston to Ponsonby, 31 August 1848, E. Ashley, *The Life of Henry John Temple, Viscount Palmerston, 1846–65, with Selections from his Speeches and Correspondence*, 2 vols (London: R. Bentley, 1876) vol. I, pp. 101–10; Southgate, p. 232.
34. Southgate, '*The Most English Minister*', pp. 232–3.
35. 3 *Hansard*, CVII, 809.
36. For a detailed treatment of Palmerston's response to the 1848 German revolution, see Frank G. Weber, 'Palmerston and Prussian Liberalism, 1848', *Journal of Modern History*, XXXV, no. 2 (1963), 50.
37. Palmerston to Lord Cowley, 1st Earl of Wellesley, 8 September, 1848, quoted in Southgate, '*The Most English Minister*', p. 227.
38. Palmerston to Victoria, 18 November 1848, in Connell (ed.), *Regina v. Palmerston*, pp. 155–6.
39. Bulwer, vol. III, pp. 407–8.
40. Palmerston to Lyons, 2 February 1848, *Parliamentary Papers, Greek Papers*, LVII.105, mf. 55.473.
41. Ridley, *Lord Palmerston*, p. 383.
42. 3 *Hansard*, CXI, 1401–4.
43. 3 *Hansard*, CXII, 380–444.
44. 3 *Hansard*, CXII, 106.
45. Connell (ed.), *Regina v. Palmerston*, pp. 74, 96–7, 102–4, 113, 115–17, 133.
46. Palmerston to Normanby, 24 January 1851, Broadlands Papers, PP/GC/NO/566.
47. Victoria to Palmerston, 6 October 1851, in Connell (ed.), *Regina v. Palmerston*, p. 102; Russell to Palmerston, 19 December 1851, and Palmerston to Russell, 23 December 1851, Bulwer, vol. IV, pp. 17, 297–9, 307–8.
48. 3 *Hansard*, CXIX, 550–77, 874–6.

Chapter 4: Politics without Party

1. Hawkins, *British Party Politics*, p. 48.
2. Memorandum of Prince Albert, 22 February 1852, *Victoria's Letters*, vol. II, p. 369.
3. Palmerston to William Temple, 30 April 1852, Broadlands Papers, PP/GC/TE/343–4, and Palmerston to Fitzwilliam, 24 September 1852, Broadlands Papers, PP/GC/FI/12–13.
4. Ridley, *Lord Palmerston*, pp. 403–4.
5. Hawkins, *British Party Politics*, p. 48.
6. Ibid., p. 52; Southgate, *The Passing of the Whigs* (New York: St Martin's, 1962) pp. 233–7.
7. Hawkins, *British Party Politics*, p. 52; Southgate, '*The Most English Minister*', p. 315.
8. Palmerston to Sulivan, 24 December 1852, Broadlands Papers, PP/GC/SU/34.
9. Broadlands Papers, PP/GC/SU/34.
10. E. D. Steele, *Palmerston and Liberalism, 1855–1865* (Cambridge: Cambridge Univeristy Press, 1991) p. 5.
11. Antony Taylor provides a survey of historians' views of Palmerston's relationship with the working classes in 'Palmerston and Radicalism, 1847–1865', *Journal of British Studies*, XXXIII: 2(April 1994) 157–79.
12. Ibid., pp. 161–7, 179.
13. Broadlands Papers, PP/GC/SU/34.
14. 3 *Hansard*, CXXIX, 1601.
15. 3 *Hansard*, CXXXV, 1306–18.
16. 3 *Hansard*, CXXV, 1209, 1210, 1213.
17. It is worth noting that when newspaper postage was based on weight, the heavier *Times* decreased its circulation (Bentley, *Politics without Democracy*, p. 151.)
18. Palmerston to Aberdeen, 10 February 1853, BL Add. MS 43049.
19. Seton-Watson, *Britain in Europe*, pp. 219–20.
20. Ibid., pp. 304–7.
21. Quoted in Southgate, '*The Most English Minister*', p. 324.
22. Llewellan Woodward, *The Age of Reform, 1815–1870* (New York: Oxford University Press, 1962) p. 254.
23. Ridley, *Lord Palmerston*, p. 417.
24. Palmerston to Aberdeen, 1 November 1853, BL Add. MS 43069.
25. Palmerston to Lansdowne, 8 December 1853, BL Add. MS 43069.
26. Palmerston to Aberdeen, 10 December 1853, BL Add. MS 43069.
27. Seton-Watson, *Britain in Europe*, p. 320.
28. Ridley, *Lord Palmerston*, p. 421.
29. Palmerston to Aberdeen, 23 December 1853, BL Add. MS 43069.

30. Broadlands Papers, PP/CAB/65–9; J. B. Conacher, *The Aberdeen Coalition, 1852–55: A Study in Mid-Nineteenth Century Party Politics* (Cambridge: Cambridge University Press, 1968) pp. 256–7.
31. Southgate, *'The Most English Minister'*, p. 349.
32. Southgate, *The Passing of the Whigs*, p. 257.
33. Ridley, *Lord Palmerston*, p. 433.
34. *Victoria's Letters*, vol. III, pp. 99–102.
35. Palmerston to Derby, 31 January 1855, Bulwer, vol. V, pp. 73–5, and Ashley, *The Life of Henry John Temple*, vol. II, pp. 76–7.
36. Hawkins, *British Party Politics*, p. 57.
37. Palmerston to Panmure, 1 and 8 May 1855, BL Add. MS 48579.
38. 3 *Hansard*, CXXXVI, 1514–39.
39. Palmerston to Clarendon, 23 November 1855, BL Add. MS 48579.
40. Broadlands Papers, PP/GC/TE/352–72.
41. Quoted in Seton-Watson, *Britain in Europe*, p. 346.
42. Palmerston to Clarendon, 25 February 1856, BL Add. MS 48580.
43. Ridley, *Lord Palmerston*, p. 451.
44. Palmerston to Clarendon, 25 February 1856, BL Add. MS 48680.
45. Ridley, *Lord Palmerston*, p. 451.
46. Ibid., p. 451.
47. Steele, *Palmerston and Liberalism*, p. 45.
48. Conacher, *The Aberdeen Coalition*, pp. 550–3.
49. Ridley, *Lord Palmerston*, p. 453; Steele, *Palmerston and Liberalism*, p. 45.
50. 3 *Hansard*, CXLIV, 1140–53; Connell (ed.), *Regina v. Palmerston*, pp. 208–11; Southgate, *'The Most English Minister'*, p. 421.
51. Palmerston to Granville, 24 and 25 March 1857, in Bell, *Lord Palmerston*, vol. II, p. 170; Hawkins, *British Party Politics*, p. 63.
52. Southgate, *'The Most English Minister'*, p. 405.
53. Palmerston to Elliott, 26 February 1841, *Parliamentary Papers, Opium Papers*, XXXVI.557, mf. 43.269–70.
54. 3 *Hansard*, CXLVI, 1831.
55. *The Times*, 24 March 1857.
56. Quoted in Ridley, *Lord Palmerston*, p. 470.
57. Quoted in Steele, *Palmerston and Liberalism*, p. 334.
58. Quoted in ibid., p. 336.
59. Hawkins, *British Party Politics*, p. 65; Ridley, *Lord Palmerston*, p. 481.
60. Steele, *Palmerston and Liberalism*, 336.

Chapter 5: The Last Years

1. Southgate, *'The Most English Minister'*, p. 443.
2. T. A. Jenkins (ed.), *The Parliamentary Diaries of Sir John Trelawny, 1858–1865*, p. 55.

3. Ibid., p. 65.
4. *Victoria's Letters*, vol. III, pp. 300, 301.
5. Quoted in Southgate, 'The Most English Minister', p. 448.
6. Palmerston to Lansdowne, 8 December 1853, mentioned in *Victoria's Letters*, vol. II, p. 465, note 2.
7. 3 *Hansard*, CLIII, 1257–61; Hawkins, *British Party Politics*, p. 74.
8. Seton-Watson, *Britain in Europe*, p. 383.
9. Quoted in Southgate, 'The Most English Minister', p. 448.
10. An account of the Tiverton election (29 April 1859), Broadlands Papers, PP/D1; Southgate, 'The Most English Minister', p. 454.
11. Hawkins, *Britain in Europe*, p. 74.
12. Russell to Graham, 17 May 1859, and Russell to Graham, 26 May 1859, in Charles Parker (ed.), *Life and Letters of Sir James Graham* (London: John Murray, 1907) vol. II, pp. 384–8.
13. Palmerston Diary, 6 June 1859, Broadlands Papers, PP/D/19.
14. Hawkins, *British Party Politics*, p. 77; Steele, *Palmerston and Liberalism*, p. 93; Southgate, 'The Most English Minister', p. 455.
15. Steele, *Palmerston and Liberalism*, pp. 118–20.
16. Russell Papers, PRO 30/22/13G; Steele, *Palmerston and Liberalism*, pp. 92–3.
17. 3 *Hansard*, CLIV, 416–421.
18. Cobden to Sale, 4 July 1859, in John Morley, *The Life of Richard Cobden* (London: T. Fisher Unwin, 1903), vol. II, pp. 229–4.
19. An account of the Tiverton election (29 April 1859), Broadlands Papers, PP/D1.
20. Palmerston to Persigny, 13 July 1859, quoted in Southgate, 'The Most English Minister', p. 463.
21. Southgate, 'The Most English Minister', p. 463.
22. 3 *Hansard*, CLVIII, 1545–8.
23. Palmerston to Gladstone, 14 April 1861, and Gladstone to Palmerston, 14 April 1861, in P. Guedalla (ed.), *The Palmerston Papers: Gladstone and Palmerston, 1851–1865* (London: Victor Gollanez, 1928) pp. 166–7
24. Steele, *Palmerston and Liberalism*, p. 104.
25. Lewis to Clarendon, 18 June 1860, noted in Palmerston's diary, Broadland's Papers, D/20.
26. Palmerston to Russell, 17 May 1860, BL Add. MS 48581, and Palmerston to Russell, 10 July 1860, BL Add. MS 48581.
27. Russell's dispatch to James Hudson, British ambassador in Turin, in G.P. Gooch (ed.), *Selections from the Speeches of Earl Russell, 1817 to 1841 and from Dispatches, 1859–1865* (London: Longmans, Green, 1870) vol. II, pp. 328–32.
28. Palmerston to Russell, 26 October 1860, Russell Papers, PRO 30/22/21.
29. The proposal ultimately foundered on the ministers' fear of affronting Austria. See Palmerston's memorandum to the Cabinet, 5 January 1860, Broadlands Papers, CAB/103.
30. Bulwer to Palmerston, 6 January 1850, and Palmerston to Bulwer, 8 March 1850, BL Add. MS 48576.

31. Palmerston's minute, 20 October 1861, BL Add. MS 38987.
32. Ibid.
33. Palmerston to Victoria, 5 December 1861, in Connell, p. 311.
34. Bell, vol. II, pp. 315–17.
35. 6 October 1861, quoted in Bell, vol. II, p. 293.
36. Palmerston to Russell, 18 October 1861, Ashley, vol. II, pp. 210–11.
37. Palmerston memorandum, 11 December 1860, Russell's Papers, PRO 30/22/21, and Palmerston to Russell, 14 September 1862, PRO 30/22/14D.
38. Palmerston to the King of Belgium, 13 March 1863, Ashley, vol. II, p. 232.
39. Bell, vol. II, p. 350.
40. Palmerston to King Leopold, 15 November 1863, Ashley, vol. II, pp. 236–42.
41. Seton-Watson, *Britain in Europe*, p. 438.
42. 3 *Hansard*, CXXII, 1252.
43. Seton-Watson, *Britain in Europe*, p. 440; Bell, vol. II, p. 366.
44. Bell, vol. II, p. 366; Southgate, 'The Most Engish Minister', pp. 509–10.
45. Quoted in Seton-Watson, *Britain in Europe*, p. 443.
46. 4 January 1864, in G. C. Buckley (ed.), *The Letters of Queen Victoria: A Selection from Her Majesty's Correspondence and Journals between 1862 and 1878*, 2nd series (London: John Murray, 1926) vol. I, pp. 140–1 [hereafter cited as *The Letters of Queen Victoria*].
47. Southgate, 'The Most English Minister', pp. 508–10; Palmerston to Russell, 26 December 1863, in Spencer Walpole, *The Life of Lord John Russell* (London: Longmans, Green, 1891) vol. II, p. 401.
48. Palmerston to Russell, 13 February 1864, Ashley, pp. 247–8.
49. Seton-Watson, *Britain in Europe*, p. 446; Russell to Victoria, 13 April 1864, *The Letters of Queen Victoria*, vol. I, pp. 168–70.
50. 3 *Hansard*, CLXXVI, 725–50, 1274–82, 1300–05.
51. Southgate, 'The Most English Minister', p. 518; Palmerston to Russell, 13 September 1865, Ashley, vol. II, pp. 270–1.
52. Bell, vol. II, p. 394; Southgate, 'The Most English Minister', pp. 525–6.
53. Palmerston to Gladstone, 11 and 12 May 1864, Guedalla, *Palmerston Papers*, 279–84.
54. Gladstone to Palmerston, 13 and 21 May 1864, Guedalla, *Palmerston Papers*, p. 285.
55. Steele, *Palmerston and Liberalism*, frontispiece, pp. 232–34, 240.
56. Bell, vol. II, p. 401; Palmerston to Victoria, 20 January 1865, *The Letters of Queen Victoria*, vol. I, pp. 248–9.
57. Quoted in Southgate, 'The Most English Minister', p. 528.
58. 3 *Hansard*, CXLVIII, 1331.
59. Brand to Palmerston, 1 June 1861, Broadlands Papers, GC/BR/12/2, and Brand to Palmerston, 31 June 1861, Broadlands Papers, GC/BR/12/2.
60. Palmerston to G. C. Lewis, 18 March 1858, Broadlands Papers, GC/LE/202.
61. Steele, *Palmerston and Liberalism*, p. 434, note 20.

62. Bell, vol. II, p. 407, note 16; 3 *Hansard*, CXXXVIII, 167–71, and 3 *Hansard*, CLXIV, 240–51.
63. Nigel Scotland, *'Good and Proper Men': Lord Palmerston and the Bench of Bishops* (Cambridge: James Clarke, 2000) pp. 5, 27.
64. Steele, *Palmerston and Liberalism*, pp. 179–80; Scotland, 'Good and Proper Men', pp. 139, 143.
65. Steele, *Palmerston and Liberalism*, p. 180.
66. Ibid., Appendix 2, p. 370; *McCalmont's Parliamentary Poll Book*, p. 294.
67. Southgate, *'The Most English Minister'*, p. 541.

Conclusion

1. John Morley, *The Life of William Ewart Gladstone* (London: Macmillan, 1903) vol. II, pp. 151–2.

BIBLIOGRAPHY

Manuscript Sources

Aberdeen Papers (British Library)
Bright Papers (British Library)
Broadlands Papers (Papers of the Third Viscount Palmerston: Southampton University Library)
Brougham Papers (Papers of Henry Brougham, University College London)
Cobden Papers (British Library)
Foreign Office Papers (Public Record Office)
Gladstone Papers (British Library)
Grey Papers (Department of Paleography, University of Durham)
Lamb Papers (British Library)
Layard Papers (British Library)
Palmerston Letter Books (British Library)
Russell Papers (Public Record Office)

Official Publications

Great Britain, Parliament, *Hansard's Parliamentary Debates*.
Parliamentary Papers, Greek Papers, vol. LVII.105, mf. 55.473.
Parliamentary Papers, Opium Papers, vol. XXXVI.557, mf. 43.269–70.

Other Sources in the Text and Notes

Ashley, E., *The Life of Henry John Temple, Viscount Palmerston, 1846–65, with Selections from his Speeches and Correspondence*, 2 vols (London: R. Bentley, 1876).

Bell, H. F. C., *Lord Palmerston*, 2 vols (London: Longmans, Green, 1936).

Benson, A. C. and Viscount Esher (eds), *The Letters of Queen Victoria: A Selection of Her Majesty's Correspondence between 1837 and 1861*, 1st series, 3 vols (London: John Murray, 1908).

Bentley, Michael, *Politics without Democracy, 1815–1914: Perceptions and Preoccupations in British Government* (London: Fontana Press, 1996).

Bourne, Kenneth, *Palmerston: The Early Years, 1784–1841* (New York: Macmillan, 1982).

Bourne, Kenneth (ed.), *The Letters of the Third Viscount Palmerston to Laurence and Elizabeth Sulivan, 1804–1863*, Camden, 4th series, vol. XXIII (London: Royal Historical Society, 1979).

Briggs, Asa, *The Age of Improvement, 1783–1867* (London: Longmans, Green, 1959).

Buckley, G. C. (ed.), *The Letters of Queen Victoria: A Selection from Her Majesty's Correspondence and Journals between 1862 and 1878*, 2nd series (London: John Murray, 1926).

Bulwer, Sir H. L. (Lord Dalling and Bulwer), *The Life of Henry John Temple, Viscount Palmerston, with Selections from his Diaries and Correspondence*, 3 vols (London: R. Bentley, 1870–4).

Chamberlain, Muriel E., *Lord Palmerston* (Washington, DC: Catholic University Press, 1987).

Conacher, J. B., *The Aberdeen Coalition, 1852–55: A Study in Mid-Nineteenth Century Party Politics* (Cambridge: Cambridge University Press, 1968).

Connell, B. (ed.), *Regina v. Palmerston: The Correspondence between Queen Victoria and her Foreign and Prime Minister, 1837–65* (London: Evans, 1902).

Czartoryski, Prince Adam, *Memoirs of Prince Adam Czartoryski*, ed. A. Guilgud (New York: Arno Press, 1971).

Edsel, Nicholas, *Richard Cobden* (Cambridge, Mass.: Harvard Unversity Press, 1986).

Edwards, R. D. and Williams, T. D. (eds), *The Great Famine: Studies in Irish History, 1845–1852* (New York: New York University Press, 1956).

Evans, Eric, *The Forging the Modern State: Early Industrial Britain, 1783–1870*, 2nd edn (London: Longman, 1996).

Gooch, G. P. (ed.), *Selections from the Speeches of Earl Russell, 1817 to 1841 and from Dispatches, 1859–1865* (London: Longmans, Green, 1870).

Guedalla, P. (ed.), *The Palmerston Papers: Gladstone and Palmerston, 1851–1865* (London: Victor Gollancz, 1928).

Hawkins, Angus, *British Party Politics, 1852–1886* (Basingstoke: Palgrave Macmillan, 1998).

Jenkins, T. A. (ed.), *The Parliamentary Diaries of Sir John Trelawny, 1858–1865*, Camden, 4th series, vol. 40 (London: Royal Historical Society, 1990).

Jones, E. Parry (ed.), *The Correspondence of Lord Aberdeen to Princess Lieven, 1832–1854*, Camden, 3rd series, vol. LX (London: Royal Historical Society, 1938).

Koss, Stephen, *The Rise and Fall of the Political Press in Britain*, vol. 1: *The Nineteenth Century* (Chapel Hill: University of North Carolina Press, 1981).
Malmesbury, the 3rd Earl (ed.), *Malmesbury Letters: A Series of Letters of the First Earl of Malmesbury and his Family and Friends, from 1745 to 1820* (London: R. Bentley, 1870).
Mitchell, A., *The Whigs in Opposition, 1815–1830* (Oxford: Clarendon Press, 1967).
Morley, John, *The Life of Richard Cobden* (London: T. Fisher Unwin, 1903).
Morley, John, *The Life of William Ewart Gladstone* (London: Macmillan, 1903).
Parker, Charles (ed.), *Life and Letters of Sir James Graham*, 2 vols (London: John Murray, 1907).
Parry, Jonathan, *The Rise and Fall of Liberal Government in Victorian Britain* (New Haven, Conn.: Yale University Press, 1993).
Reid, Stuart (ed.), *Durham: The Life and Letters of the First Earl Durham, 1792–1840* (London: Longmans, Green, 1906).
Ridley, Jasper, *Lord Palmerston* (New York: E. P. Dutton, 1971).
Royle, Trevor, *Crimea: The Great Crimean War, 1854–1856* (New York: St Martin's Press, 2000.
Scotland, Nigel, *'Good and Proper Men': Lord Palmerston and the Bench of Bishops* (Cambridge: James Clarke, 2000).
Seton-Watson, R. W., *Britain in Europe, 1789–1914: A Survey of Foreign Policy* (Cambridge: Cambridge University Press, 1955).
Southgate, Donald, *The Passing of the Whigs* (New York: St Martin's, 1962).
Southgate, Donald, *'The Most English Minister...': The Policies and Politics of Palmerston* (London: Macmillan, 1966).
Steele, E. D., *Palmerston and Liberalism, 1855–1865* (Cambridge: Cambridge University Press, 1991).
Vincent, J. and Stinton, M. (ed.), *McCalmont's Parliamentary Poll Book: British Election Results, 1832–1918*, 8th edn (Brighton: Harvester Press, 1971).
Walpole, Spencer, *The Life of Lord John Russell*, 2 vols (London: Longmans, Green, 1891).
Webster, C. K., *Foreign Policy of Palmerston, 1830–1841: Britain, the Liberal Movement and the Eastern Question*, 2 vols (London: G. Bell, 1951).
Woodward, Llewellan, *The Age of Reform, 1815–1870* (New York: Oxford University Press, 1962).

Journal Articles

Anbinder, Tyler, 'Lord Palmerston and the Irish Famine Emigration', *The Historical Journal*, XLIV: 2 (2001) 441–69.
Aspinall, Arthur, 'The Formation of the Goderich Ministry', *English Historical Review*, XLII (1927) 533–59.

Bradfield, B. T., 'Sir Richard Vyvyan and the Fall of the Wellington Government', *Historical Journal*, XI (1968), 141–56.

Davis, Richard W., 'Wellington and the "Open Question": the Issue of Catholic Emancipation, 1821–1829', *Albion*, 29: 1 (Spring, 1997) pp. 39–55.

Golicz, Roman, 'Napoleon III, Lord Palmerston and the *Entente Cordiale*', *History Today*, vol. 12 (December 2000), 10–17.

Taylor, Antony, 'Palmerston and Radicalism, 1847–1865', *Journal of British Studies*, XXXIII: 2 (April 1994) 157–79.

Weber, Frank G., 'Palmerston and Prussian Liberalism, 1848', *Journal of Modern History*, XXXV, no. 2 (1963) 125–36.

INDEX

Since Palmerston is mentioned throughout the text, there is no entry for him in the index.

1848 revolutions, 5, 65, 72, 85, 88, 111, 130, 131
Aberdeen, Lord, 5, 7, 58, 62–3, 80, 81, 85–9, 92, 96–7
Aberdeen Coalition, 84, 91, 96
Act of Union (1801), 5, 7, 59, 125
Afghan War (1838–42), 51
Albert, Prince, 63–4, 73, 76, 89, 115, 118
Alexander I, Tsar, 9
Alexander II, Tsar, 94, 103, 116–17
Almacks Club, 16, 29, 108
Althorp, Lord, 8, 39
America, 5, 58
American Civil War, 114–15
American Confederacy, 115–16
American War of Independence, 58
Anglican Church, 126–7
Anti-Corn Law League, 56–7; *see also* Corn Laws; free trade; protectionism
Anti-Slavery Society, 19, 59
Apsley House Agreement, 21
Arrow, the, 99
Ashburton, Lord, 58
Ashley, Lord Anthony, 58–9, 83; *see also* Shaftsbury, Earl

Baines, Edward, 122, 126–7
Bankes, Henry, 19
Bases de Separation, 31, 32

Bathurst, Lord, 19
Battle of Antietam, 116
Battle of Bull Run, 115
Battle of Gettysburg, 116
Bedchamber Crisis (1839), 52
Belgian Treaty, 128
Bell, Herbert, 12
Benedict XVI, Pope, 35
Berlin Decree (1806), 9
Bismarck, Otto von, 117–20, 132
Blanc, Louis, 68
Bolivar, Simon, 17
Bonaparte, Emperor Napoleon, 7, 10, 17; *see also* Bonapartism; Napoleonic wars
Bonapartism, 3
Bourne, Kenneth, 12
Brand, Henry, 125
Bright, John, 3, 98, 100, 106, 109, 115, 123, 127
Broadlands, 15, 56
Brocket Park, 128
Brooks Club, 87
Brougham, Lord Henry, 8
Bulwer, H. L., 62, 74
Buol, Count Heinrich, 94
Burdett, Sir Francis, 18, 19
Burke, Edmund, 7

Cadiz, Duke of, 62
Cambridge University, 8–9, 19, 121

151

Index

Cambridge constituency, 18–19, 40
Canning, George, 2, 9–10, 16–18, 20–1, 40, 53, 56, 130; *see also* Canningites
Canning, Stratford, 86, 88; *see also* Stratford de Redcliffe
Canningites, 2, 19, 21–3, 39, 47, 54, 58
Carlists, 45
Carlos, Don, 43–4
Caroline, Queen, 14–16
Castlereagh, Lord, 3, 10–11, 16, 25, 34, 38, 45, 130
Catholic Association, 17, 23
Catholic Emancipation, 2, 4, 7, 9, 17–19, 23–5, 129
Catholic Question, 8, 11, 18, 20–1, 23
Cato Street conspiracy (1820), 14
Cavaignac, General Louis, 68
Cavendish, William, 40
Cavour, Camillo di, 107, 113
Charles Albert, King, 67, 69, 73
Chartists, 52, 55, 59, 64–5, 82, 115
Christian IV, King, 118
Christian of Glucksberg, Duke, 119
Christian VII, King, 71
Church of England, 126, 127; *see also* Anglican Church
Civis Romanus Sum speech, 75
Clarence, Duke of, 20, 26; *see also* William IV
Clarendon, Lord, 81, 84, 86, 92, 94–5
Clayton–Bulwer Treaty (1850), 114
Cobden, Richard, 3, 56, 87, 98, 100, 09
Cobdenites, 109, 121
Collective Note (1839), 49
Concert of Europe, 25, 59
Concert Powers, 16–17, 95
Congress of Paris (1856), 94–7, 118
Congress of Verona (1822), 17
Congress of Vienna (1815), 14, 30, 36–8, 59, 64, 68, 95

Congress System, 34, 71
Conservatives, 128; *see also* Tories
Conspiracy to Murder Bill (1858), 102
Copenhagen expedition, 10
Copley, John, 19
Corn Laws, 19–20, 22, 57, 78; *see also* Anti-Corn Law League; free trade; protectionism
Cowper, Earl, 16
Cowper, Lady Emily, 16, 52; *see also* Lady Palmerston
Cowper, Minnie, 58
Crimean War, 84–5, 90, 93, 95–7, 99, 130
Croker, Sir John, 27
Czartoryski, Prince Adam, 37

De Lancey, Lt General Oliver, 13
De Redcliffe, Lord Stratford, 86, 88
Declaration of Paris (1856), 96
Delane, John, 76
Denison, Sir William, 101
Derby, Edward Stanley, Lord, 27, 75, 77–81, 92, 98, 102, 105–6, 109, 128
Derbyites, 93, 98, 100, 107, 109–10, 132
Devon and Cornwall Mining Company, 20
Disraeli, Benjamin, 57, 80, 98, 105, 107, 121, 128
Dissenters, 126–7
Dudley, Lord, 20–1, 23
Dumas, Alexander, 61
Dundas, General David, 13
Durham, Lord, 39, 43
Dutch Union (1815), 30

East India Company, 100, 101
Eastern Powers, 33, 34, 36, 38, 44–6, 49, 62–7

Index

Eastern Question, 21, 46, 48, 87, 96
Easthorpe, John, 56
Eldon, Lord, 19
Ellice, Edward, 43
Elliott, Sir Gilbert, 66–7
Emancipation Proclamation (1863), 116
Endowed Schools Act (1860), 127
entente cordiale, 4, 62–3
Espartero, General Baldomero, 45
Esterhazy, Prince, 32,
Evans, Colonel de Lacey, 41
Exaltados, 62

Factory Acts, 82
Fenians, 125
Ferdinand II of Naples, King, 70
Ferdinand VII of Spain, King, 17
Foreign Enlistment Act (1819), 45
Four Points of 1854, 96
Fox, Charles James, 7, 11
Foxites, 7, 53
Frederick William, King
free trade, 4, 79; *see also*
  Anti Corn Law League;
  Corn Laws; protectionism
French Revolution (1789), 1, 7, 67
French Revolution (1830), 29, 34;
  see also July Revolution
French Revolution (1848), 67

Garibaldi, Guiseppe, 69, 113–14, 121–2
George III, 7, 9, 11–12, 14, 17
George IV, King, 15–16, 20–1, 25–6
German Diet's Six Resolutions, 37, 57, 59
German Federal Diet, 118–19
Germanic Confederation, 118–19
Gibson, Thomas Milner, 102, 109, 111

Gladstone, William, 80–2, 106, 109–16, 122–4, 128–9, 133
Globe, 56, 84, 89
Goderich, Frederick Robinson, Lord, 21
Gorchakov, Prince Alexander, 94
Goulborn, Henry, 19, 40
Graham, Sir James, 42, 88, 92
Grant, Charles, 20–2, 26
Granville, Baron Granville Leveson–Gower, 31, 46
Great Powers, 29, 30, 33, 50, 67, 97, 131
Grenville ministry, 7; *see also*
  Ministry of All the Talents
Grenville, William, 9
Greville, Charles, 76
Grey, Lord Charles, 4, 10, 27, 40
Grey Ministry, 26, 28, 39
Guizot, François, 16, 50, 61–4, 66, 76

Habeas Corpus Act, 14
Halevy, Elie, 48
Hambach Festival (1832), 37
Hapsburg, 35, 70
Harney, G. J., 65
Hawkins, Angus, 80
Haynau, General, 69–70
Herbert, Sidney, 92
Herries, John, 21
Holland, Lord, 27, 50
Holy Places, 85
House of Oldenburg, 119
Hugo, Victor, 61
Hume, Joseph, 14, 36, 41
Huskisson, William, 19–23, 25–6
Huskissonians, 26

Ibrahim, 48
India Act (1858), 101–2, 105
Irish Famine, 6–1, 125
Industrial Revolution, 1, 4, 7, 54, 82

Index

Irish Established Church, 126, 127
Irish Coercion Bill (1833), 42
Isabella II, 43–6, 62–3
Isbelinos, 45

Jackson, Andrew, 58
Jersey, Lady, 15
Johnians, 8
July Revolution, 29; see also French Revolution (1830)

Kossuth, Louis, 70, 82–4

Lamartine, Alphonse de, 68
Lamb, Emily 16; see also Cowper, Lady Emily; Palmerston, Lady
Lansdowne, Marquis of, 8, 27, 79, 81
Layard, Henry, 93, 97, 100
Lee, General Robert E., 116
Leeds Mercury, 127
Leopold Saxe-Coburg, Prince, 31–2, 63
Leuchtenberg, Duke of, 31
Lewis, George Cornewall, 97, 110, 113
Liberal Party, 3, 54, 81–2, 109, 111, 130, 132–3
Liberals, 98, 106, 109, 128, 130–1
Liberation Society, 98, 127
Lieven, Ambassador Christopher, 33
Lieven, Princess, 15, 27, 62, 76, 109
Lincoln, Abraham, 114–15
Liverpool, Lord, 8, 14, 16, 18–20
Liverpool Ministry, 2, 17, 21
London Conference (1830), 29–4, 30–6
Louis Philippe, 4, 30–1, 35, 45, 53, 62–3, 131
Luddite riots, 14
Luisa, Princess, 62–3

Mahmud II, Sultan, 46–9
Malmesbury, Third Earl, 12
Manchester School of Liberalism, 98, 109, 115
Maria Christina, Queen, 43, 45, 62–3
Maria II da Gloria, Queen, 17, 24–5, 43–4, 46, 64
Marx, Karl, 87
Mason, James, 115
Mazzini, Guiseppe, 102, 121
Mehemet Ali, 47–1, 57, 130
Melbourne, Lord William, 4, 26–7, 39, 43, 50, 52, 57
Menshikov, Prince Alexander, 86
Metternich, Prince, 16, 33, 35, 37, 39, 68, 70
Miguel, Don, 24–5, 43–4
Militia Bill (1852), 77, 78
Mill, John Stuart, 124
Ministry of All the Talents, 7; see also Grenville ministry
Monroe Doctrine, 17
Montpensier, Duke of, 63
Morning Chronicle, 57–8, 84
Morning Post, 56, 84, 89, 115

Napier, Sir Charles, 44
Napoleon I, 7, 10, 17, 97; see also Bonapartism; Napoleonic wars
Napoleon III, Emperor, 76, 84, 94–6, 102, 107–8, 111–14, 117, 119, 121
Napoleonic Wars, 9
National Workshops, 68
Nelson, Horatio, 7
Nemours, Duke of, 31
Nesselrode, Count, 75
Netherlands, 30, 32
New Poor Law, 3–4, 52, 57
Newcastle, Duke of, 90–1, 96, 110
Newport Rising (1839), 65
Nicholas I, Tsar, 85–7, 90

Nightingale, Florence, 91
Normanby, Lord Contantine, 76

O'Connell, Daniel, 4, 17, 23–4, 36, 52
Opium War, 51
Orlov, Count Alexis, 94–5
Orsini, Felicini, 102
Orsini Plot, 102

Pacifico, Don, 3, 24, 73–5, 77–8, 100, 130
Palmerston, Lady, 61; *see also* Lamb, Emily
Palmerstonianism, 4, 82, 102, 133
Papal States, 35–6, 67
Parliamentary Reform Bill (1832), 4, 39–41, 52, 5, 87, 96, 106
Pedro, Don, 44
Peel, Sir Robert, 16, 20–1, 24–5, 40, 56–7, 61
Peelites, 79–81, 91–3, 98, 100, 102
Penal Servitude Bill (1853), 83
Peninsular War, 10, 15
Percival, Spencer, 8, 10–13
Peterloo Massecre (1819), 2, 65
Petty, Lord Henry, 8
Philip II, King, 30
Pitt, Sir William, 7–8, 11
Pittites, 8
Pius IX, Pope, 67, 69
Place, Francis, 40
Portland, Duke of, 7, 9–10
Prince of Orange, 31
protectionism, 57, 79; *see also* Anti Corn Law League; Corn Laws; free trade
Protocol of 20 December (1830), 30

Quadruple Alliance (1833), 44–6, 49, 62–3, 65, 130–1
Quarterly Review, 106

Radetzky, General Josef, 69–70
radicals, 40–1, 49, 52, 66, 98, 109, 126
Raglan, Lord, 91
Realpolitik, 120–1
Red Shirts, 69, 113
Reform Club, 81
Reformatory Schools Bill (1854), 83
Richmond, Duke of, 24
Ridley, Jasper, 38
Roebuck, J. A., 56, 75, 87, 92, 96, 102, 133
Roman Republic, 69
Rowcliffe, 79
Russell, Lord John, 4, 61, 73, 76, 78, 84, 87, 92, 98, 106–7, 110–11, 113
Russell, William Howard, 91
Ryder Street Committee, 98

Second French Republic (1848), 68
Sepoy Mutiny (1857), 100–1
Septembrists, 64
Seville, Duke of, 62
Seward, William, 115
Shaftsbury, Earl of, 58, 83, 100, 126–7; *see also* Ashley, Anthony
Sidmouth, Lord, 10, 14
Six Acts, 2, 14, 65
slave trade, 4, 115
slave trade abolition, 4, 8, 52
Slidell, John, 115
Sligo, 18, 59–60, 124
Smoke Abatement Bill (1853), 82
Sonderbund, 66
Southgate, Donald, 12, 38, 40, 120
Spa Field Riots (1816), 14
Spanish Civil War, 62
Spencer, Earl, 8
Stanley, Lord Edward, 27, 75; *see also* Derby
Staunton, Sir George, 42

Steele, E. D., 81–2, 112, 123–4, 132
Straits Convention (1841), 50–1, 85–6
Stratford de Redcliffe, 86, 88; *see also* Canning, Stratford
Sulivan, Laurence, 81
Swiss Confederation, 66

Talavera, 10
Talleyrand, Charles, 29, 32
Taylor, Antony, 81–2
Taylor, Sir Brooke, 35
Temple, William, 21, 94
Ten Hours Bill (1844), 59
Test Acts, 9, 24
Thiers, Adolphe, 50, 61
Times, The, 20, 56, 84, 96, 115, 117
Tiverton constituency, 43, 52, 65, 79, 81, 107–8, 127–8
Tories, 8, 16, 41, 45, 52, 63, 79, 97, 102, 107, 128
Tory Party, 4, 16, 19, 21–2, 40, 61, 78, 80, 92, 133
Trafalgar, Battle of, 7, 9
Treaty of Adrianople, 47
Treaty of Kutchuk Kainardji (1774), 85
Treaty of London (1852), 118–19
Treaty of Nanking (1842), 52, 99
Treaty of Paris (1783), 58
Treaty of Tilsit (1807), 9
Treaty of Unkiar Skelessi (1833), 48, 50
Treaty of Utrecht (1713), 62–3
Treaty of Villafranca (1859), 111
Trelawny, John, 105
Trent (British steamer), 115–16

Urquhart, David, 139

Victor Emmanuel, King, 69, 111, 113
Victoria, 52, 63–4, 68–9, 73, 76–7, 80, 119, 131
Villiers, Charles, 111
Villiers, George, 84, 86; *see also* Clarendon

Wagram, 10
Walewski, Count Alexandre, 94
Waterloo, Battle of, 13
Webster, Daniel, 58
Webster–Ashburton Treaty (1842), 58
Wellesley, Arthur, 10
Wellington, Duke of, 10, 13, 17, 19–22, 24–7, 30, 40
Wellington ministry, 23, 25–6
Western Powers, 45, 90
Whigs, 2, 10, 16, 19, 40, 42, 52, 61, 78, 80, 92, 106, 132
Whiggery, 53–4
Wilberforce, William, 8
Wilhelm I, Kaiser, 119
William I, King, 31, 32
William IV, 26, 37
William of Nassau, 30–2
Willis' Rooms, 108, 110–1, 133
Wilson, General Robert, 15
Wood, Charles, 110

York, Duke of, 13, 19–20

Zollverein, 71